Advance Praise for
Searching for Michael Jackson's Nose

"What's your name again? He says he's never heard of you."
— Personal assistant to Steve Martin

"A blurb? So would he have to actually read the book?"
— Intern on the staff of *Jimmy Kimmel Live*

"Listen: I'm not even going to ask him, because I know he'll say no."   — Publicist for Jim Carrey

"How did you get this number?"
— Business manager for David Letterman

SEARCHING FOR MICHAEL JACKSON'S NOSE

NOT BY THE AUTHOR

The Lighter Side of Gandhi

Thursdays With Charo

*How to Build a Bomb Shelter from Thousands
of Remaindered Copies of Thursdays With Charo*

Idiocy for Dummies

*Love Story II: Love Means Doing the Laundry
Every Now and Then, You Fat Slob*

The Holy Bible

*Steven Hawking's Latest Book You'll Buy
but Never Actually Read*

*The Seven Habits of People Who Aren't Screwed Up
Enough to Need This Book, Unlike You*

Dear Dr. Phil: Shut Your Friggin' Piehole! Sincerely, Everyone

Gretchen Mol: Nothing's Gonna Stop Her Now!

What Stopped Gretchen Mol?

Ghost Dude

SEARCHING FOR

MICHAEL
JACKSON'S
NOSE

AND OTHER PREOCCUPATIONS
OF OUR CELEBRITY-MAD CULTURE

SCOTT FESCHUK

M&S

National Library of Canada Cataloguing in Publication

Feschuk, Scott
Searching for Michael Jackson's nose : and other preoccupations
of our celebrity-mad culture / Scott Feschuk.

ISBN 0-7710-4752-5

1. Celebrities in mass media. 2. Popular culture. I. Title.

P96.C35F47 2003   302.23'0862'1   C2003-902054-1

We acknowledge the financial support of the Government of Canada through the
Book Publishing Industry Development Program and that of the Government of
Ontario through the Ontario Media Development Corporation's Ontario Book
Initiative. We further acknowledge the support of the Canada Council for the
Arts and the Ontario Arts Council for our publishing program.

Typeset in Minion by M&S, Toronto
Printed and bound in Canada

McClelland & Stewart Ltd.
The Canadian Publishers
481 University Avenue
Toronto, Ontario
M5G 2E9
www.mcclelland.com

1 2 3 4 5   07 06 05 04 03

For Sue, James, and Will

To Laura and Dave,

You bought 3 copies
of my book and
are therefore my
new best friends.

Thanks,

Scott

CONTENTS

Acknowledgements

For her meticulous and indispensable help with this book, I owe an immense debt of gratitude to my wife, Susan Allan. What a relief, then, that we live in twenty-first-century North America, where credit lines are a societal requisite and debts don't ever need to be repaid. Sue's contribution – in inspiration, in ideas, in editing – was of such a magnitude that it will be an effort just to keep up with the payments on the interest.

Thanks also to Ken Whyte, who hired me at the *National Post*, and Tim Rostron, who suggested I write about television. Were it not for the two of them, this book would not exist, a fact I mention not only to show that I'm grateful but also to ensure my name does not appear alone on any class-action suit filed by people demanding a refund.

Some of these chapters are revised versions of columns that appeared in the *Post*. Countless mistakes, redundancies, and sultry passages in which I successfully seduced Cameron Diaz were expertly excised by my editor, Dinah Forbes, who probably also made the book much better in other ways but frankly I'm too blinded by the whole Cameron Diaz thing to see them.

Finally, thanks to my parents, Brian and Muriel Feschuk, who so expertly hide their embarrassment that their son watches television for a living.

CELEBRITIES ARE GREAT!*

1. Kels and Me

"I love eating outdoors!" Kelsey Grammer told me.

Well, I say me. What I mean is any of the fifteen million people who, like me, caught that particular episode of *InStyle* magazine's *Celebrities at Home*. Still, it felt like a private conversation. Just me and Kels – I call him Kels – sitting around his elegant, extravagant homestead. "I love eating outdoors, too," I said, just in case, and Kelsey smiled weakly. I wasn't sure if he had actually heard me or if he had just then grasped the irony of boasting about the secluded nature of his private sanctuary to a camera crew that was filming his twenty-foot ceilings and his handmade couch pillows for international broadcast in prime time. It's a recurring theme of such shows: my home is a haven, a retreat, a refuge from the oppressive world of fame and immense fortune. Only close family members and the best of friends are welcome here. But please, by all means, have your portly cameraman employ a fetishist swoop as he adoringly films the four-poster bed in which I have intercourse with my wife.

---

* Warning: Chapter Title May Contain Trace Elements of Sincerity

What would prompt a celebrity – or, more often, a *telebrity*, an actor who has a featured role on a network TV series but is, even after four seasons, most often referred to by viewers as the Guy Who Plays That Hot Chick's Dad – to appear on *InStyle Celebrities at Home*, or other programs of its fawning ilk, such as *MTV Cribs* and the lower-wattage *Celebrity Homes*, a program that is more likely to showcase the domicile of the Portly, Wisecracking Work Acquaintance of the Guy Who Plays That Hot Chick's Dad? More perplexing, what prompts us to watch?

These programs purport to offer a behind-the-scenes glimpse at what it's like to be a celebrity, just as *The Larry Sanders Show* did for a talk-show host and the arrest of Heidi Fleiss did for Charlie Sheen's penis. The shows are designed to buff the glossy patina of stardom to a hypnotic brilliance, to prompt the simple folk of America to covet the lagoon-style pool and the matching Bentleys and the limestone fireplace, bought at auction in the south of France, naturally. And I suppose it would be naive to deny that, somewhere out there, some discontented housewife is at this very moment affixing her hubby with an accusing eye, silently grouching that his utter lack of celebrity has denied her a thirty-thousand-dollar crystal vase or the gift of a jukebox from Jon Bon Jovi or a stable for their seven horses, which, come to think of it, they don't even have anyway on account of his not being on TV or in the movies and therefore not predisposed to matters equine.

Nevertheless, it's plausible that these shows are in fact clever ploys by ingenious philosophers to showcase the utter pointlessness of craving fame and wealth. Take Grammer, for instance. The guy has been in the business for two decades. He has money, celebrity, critical respect – and still he's needy and insecure enough to succumb to the urge to show America his dual massage tables and "professional" tennis court. "Kelsey's just a middle-class kid who goes to work," Kelsey said from his twenty-thousand-dollar couch, using the third-person form that apparently comes complimentary with all mansions in the greater Los Angeles area. "I like my job. I like my home. I love my wife. I love America." Presumably the director generously edited out the ensuing emotional breakdown in which a sobbing Kelsey hollered, "America likes Kelsey, right? Right? *Tell me America loves Kelsey back!*"

That was sad, but not quite as pathetic as the sight, later in that hour of *Celebrities at Home*, of actress Vivica A. Fox sporting a tank top as she sat in front of a roaring fire in her custom-built home. They must have turned off the cameras when she said, "I don't care if it is 104 degrees outside, so long as I am rich and there are fireplaces in my house, there will be a goddamn fire in my fireplace."

The proceedings on *Celebrity Homes* are routinely even more pitiable. The first episode I ever saw featured Joe Piscopo, and I remember thinking, Okay, so when are they going to tell us which famous person used to live in his house? And then I realized: Oh, they mean Joe. They mean Joe's a celebrity. *Riiiight.*

More recently, I caught an episode that profiled the living quarters of the members of the B-grade boy band O-Town.

One of the fellas lamented his hectic lifestyle, how he's always on a plane, how he no longer gets time to "chill" at home any more. It is to the eternal credit of the show's host that she resisted the urge to look at her watch and say, "Hey, give it five more minutes, pal."

This style of show isn't new, but the relentlessly worshipful tone certainly is. There was a cheeky demeanour favoured by Robin Leach on *Lifestyles of the Rich & Famous*, with his signature cry – applied to everything from George Hamilton's bathroom faucets to the fillings in Ernest Borgnine's teeth – of, "It's made from solid gold!" The producers of that show not only understood but also gently mocked our voyeuristic tendencies, our collective middle-class lust for champagne on a balcony in Monaco.

The new shows are far more likely to offer us a sober, worshipful glimpse at the formidable Italian retreat of Donatella Versace, the fashion designer who, at least while speaking in English, sounds very much like an adult on a Charlie Brown special. She, too, made *InStyle Celebrities at Home*, and the tone was reverent, pious even. Describing some of the artwork on the premises, Versace said (and I'm going from my notes here): "Waa whaaa wa wha whaaaaa."

Still, we got the point: she's spectacularly rich and we're not. How rich is she? Her family even has a logo, which is etched on its dishes and appears on furniture throughout the house. I bet Kelsey Grammer watched this episode to see how he and the missus and their eight-thousand-square-foot hilltop home came off. And I bet he immediately commissioned a

Grammer family logo. After all, what self-respecting celebrity could possibly live without one?

Not long after viewing the pristine interior of Grammer's mansion, I got to thinking about the annihilation of the human species. The catalyst: an hour spent viewing *InStyle's Celebrity Moms*.

Imagine that you're God. It's Judgement Day and you're hunkered down on the splendid white throne, ruling on the fate of billions of souls based on what has been recorded in the great books. After a time, you start to regard in the notations a rather peculiar behaviourial trend. You summon your heavenly minions: "I'm familiar with the murder and the adultery. And don't sell Me short, I'm hip to the latest perversions, too. But could one of you fill me in on this freaky obsession with the private lives of halfwit supermodels and narcissistic actors? I mean, what does anyone care how a chick from *Days of Our Lives* decorates her friggin' nursery?"

If a society can be judged by the people it reveres, we're not even going to qualify for the afterlife playoffs. Assemble a team of the planet's finest authors, Pulitzers out the wazoo. Give each a laptop, an Underwood, a pen, an Etch-a-Sketch, whatever. Permit this divine assemblage of lexiconic craftsmen to hone their prose until the commas gleam from rigorous polishing. They won't stand a chance. Nobody and nothing can mock television, and mock us for watching certain types of television, better than television itself.

The premise of *Celebrity Moms* was that celebrity moms are better and more interesting moms because they are, well, celebrities. The other premise of *Celebrity Moms* was that enough of us are sufficiently pitiable to watch enraptured as wealthy TV actresses are portrayed as heroic role models for being back on the set just three weeks after giving birth, and for bravely signing the cheques required to have someone else design and decorate their baby's bedroom. "Even for a successful TV star," we're told at one point, "the realities of motherhood are never too far away." Yes, that's true: I believe they're called "nannies."

The great joke of *Celebrity Moms* is that childbirth and the early months of motherhood are prodigious human equalizers. Babies must be born: you can't order your personal assistant to take care of the labour. And no number of leather-trimmed suede infant fedoras by Gucci can disguise the fact that a baby, unless he is your own, is a fundamentally uninteresting creation to behold.

So *Celebrity Moms* was replete with famous women saying things like, "Being pregnant isn't always easy!" and "She's my baby. She's just my baby." Well, duh. Shouldn't even the most fawning of superstar worshippers have standards? Should we not decree: we'll read the saucy gossip about your sexual dalliances; we'll buy the magazines with the fawning profiles and airbrushed pics; to heck with Judgement Day, we'll even gamely covet the physical manifestations of your immense wealth, be they your vast array of vintage roadsters or your wife's new boobies. But please don't make us watch you doing one of the few things in life that we can experience for ourselves, and do as well or better than you.

Celebrities make a pastime of bitching about the tabloids, about the relentless invasion of their sacred privacy, but what they're really bitching about is nature of the invasion. To celebrities, privacy is just another commodity to be used as a bargaining chip to perpetuate their fame. Come inside my home, come look at my baby, come read in the new issue of *Vanity Fair* all about what I really think about things. As fascinated as the world is with the star-making machinery behind the popular star, this infrastructure pales in comparison to Hollywood's star-perpetuating machinery, the industry that exists to *keep* people famous: the celebrity profiles, the celebrity versions of reality programs, the toadying interviews on *Entertainment Tonight*, and, perhaps above all else, awards shows, at which celebrities can have their celebrity enhanced by being honoured for having been such excellent celebrities. The centrepiece of the 54th Annual Emmy Awards was, you may recall, a tribute to the humanitarian exploits of Oprah Winfrey, a salute that employed so many commendatory adjectives that, the following morning, Roget's was obliged to commence production on a new batch of synonyms for "virtuous." After viewing the video reel in which A-list celebrities expressed an almost lascivious regard for Oprah's feats of do-goodery, it was something of a surprise to discover that Winfrey was actually there, *still alive* and everything, and ready to collect the inaugural Bob Hope Humanitarian Award. For a while, it seemed we were watching the world's first live canonization. (Our first clue should have been the casting: Tom Cruise, who was featured in the video reel, was all wrong as the Pope.)

This is not to belittle Oprah's benevolent initiatives, nor her mighty footprint on pop culture, nor her inarguable status as an influential role model and a first-rate megalomaniac (on the cover of this month's *Oprah* magazine . . . Oprah!). But the absurd solemnity and overwrought vocabulary of many who participated in the tribute gave the ceremony a familiar sheen of Hollywood insincerity. It was as though these celebrities were simply in awe of the fact that any of their kind would so much as lift a bejewelled middle finger in the direction of the average folk who watch their TV shows and see their movies and finance their detox stints. "Your efforts have daily lit up the darkest corners of millions of lives," Cruise said in all apparent seriousness. I'm sure Oprah was suitably moved – and then immediately began brainstorming the excellent adjectives she'd deploy when a similar honour is conferred on Cruise.

2. Obsequious Bootlicking + Famous Person = Steady Job

"The Actors Studio is proud to welcome Linda, Philip, Dieter, Simon, Lothar, Wayne, Austin, Dr. Evil, Fat Bastard . . . ," the peculiar, bespectacled man said, pausing to regain his balance after being almost washed from the stage by the tsunami of *woo-hoo*s that greeted his mention of the corpulent villain from the *Austin Powers* movies. Having towelled off, he continued owlishly, ". . . and, oh yes, Mike Myers."

The name of the television program is *Inside the Actors Studio*, a title that conjures the image of, say, Warren Beatty trying to school Freddie Prinze, Jr., and other new hot things in how to convey varying emotions and abandon the straight-ahead, confused gaze that suggests neither complexity nor conflicted duality but rather that the character can't quite decide what to order from the McDonald's menu. In practice, the series – a lengthy Q&A with a film celeb – is more commonly known as the Show Where Big Stars Are "Interviewed" by That Odd, Fawning Dweeb.

Imprisoned behind a table stacked high with blue notecards, host James Lipton said of Myers: "Tonight's guest has not only made us laugh, he has in some significant ways changed the way we think." The notoriously gushy Lipton didn't expand on this titanic platitude, and really, why bother? Sunny idolatry is the default state of the celebrity interviewer, and often of their audiences. Deathly afraid to alienate a potential future employer, the audience of film students dutifully roared at even Myers's weakest gags. One woman was glimpsed chortling with such a disturbing, face-reddening ferocity that I felt compelled to scan the closing credits for the reassuring disclaimer: "No bootlickers died during the making of this program."

As Lipton routinely demonstrates, one of the prevailing features of most celebrity interviews is the sense that both participants fancy themselves celebrities. Your Diane Sawyers, your Larry Kings, your Barbara Walterses, they interview the stars while never letting us forget that they too are stars, and this creates a peculiar dynamic.

In Lipton's mind, there are always two famous folks on the stage, and he never misses a chance to turn to the audience and inject such clumsy, puzzling remarks as "Sometimes life is just good!" Sitting across from Myers, he also couldn't resist making frequent reference to the fact he's thrice now been lampooned on *Saturday Night Live*. Lipton hasn't clued in that his belly-aching serves only to illustrate why he's so appealing a target.

Towards the end of the program, Lipton remarked, "I'm sometimes criticized for being too effusive with my guests," which is of course balderdash. He is relentlessly criticized for being too effusive with his guests, but there's no doubt his reverential manner explains why he's able to land such mighty names. Obsequious bootlicking + famous person = steady job: it's an equation that's familiar to Sawyer and King and Walters and certainly to Katie Couric, co-host of *Today* on NBC, who is paid in the order of $748 billion a year to conduct early-morning chats with cookbook authors, Scrabble champion, and recovering nymphomaniacs. In 2002, after negotiating a new contract, the much-loved television personality secured the right to produce and present the occasional prime-time special featuring genuine A-listers. The first instalment, entitled *Katie at Night*, was introduced with shots of Couric bounding perkily through Midtown Manhattan, her eyeliner slathered on in what could only be a loving homage to Alice Cooper.

The hour was comprised of interviews with three celebrities (Sharon Stone, Shania Twain, and Olivia Harrison, widow of George Harrison), a familiar format that rather plainly announced Couric's aspiration to establish herself as the definitive corporeal sequel to Walters, still the reigning queen of superstar adulation and flattering, soft-focus gauze.

The program began in San Francisco, with Couric sitting across from Stone, who a year earlier had abruptly suffered a potentially fatal trauma to her brain. I do not claim to possess an especially savvy intuition regarding the mindset of television personalities, but it seemed quite apparent to me that Katie really, really wanted Sharon to cry. *Famous people cry for Barbara, dammit! You're going to cry for me!* And to ensure that Stone did indeed make with the tears of ratings gold, Couric referenced the actress's ailment and solemnly declared, "According to the medical literature, an estimated 10 to 15 per cent of people who have what you had die before they even get to a hospital. [Stone nods.] Mortality can be as high as 40 per cent within the first week. [Stone's eyes grow moist.] About half die in the first six months. [Stone's face quivers.] Those are scary statistics! [Stone breaks down, turns her head from the camera, wipes a tear, and says, "I need to take a break."]."

Bawling at the five-minute mark of the interview: Take that, Barbara!

There is no denying that Couric has legions of fans, and although her alleged charm eludes me, I'll happily defer to the masses and accept that she's a comforting, amusing presence on a weekday morning. What is beyond debate, however, is that she has embraced the most mockable elements of the traditional celebrity interview. Rather than attempt anything so mundane as eliciting information, for instance, Couric is forever trying to impress her audience by proving that she's read the research material prepared by some flunky. From the way she avoids sentences that end in question marks, you'd think there was a global punctuation crisis. Instead of asking Shania Twain to describe her childhood, Couric *told* the singer that she was dirt poor and was awakened at cruel hours to perform at local dives. "Mm-hmm," Shania remarked. Instead of asking Olivia Harrison about the night on which a man broke into their home outside London and stabbed her husband repeatedly in the chest, Couric *told* her.

KATIE: "You might not want to admit it, but you were pretty feisty!"
OLIVIA: "Yeah."
KATIE: "You took that lamp and you walloped him over the head with it!"

Uh, thanks, Katie. But you see the poor widow sitting across from you? *She was actually there.* Go ahead, ask her about it!

Alas, it was not to be. The interview went on to produce such quotes as, "This is such a spectacular place, and George absolutely adored it" and "George had an incredible joie de vivre" – excerpts that would have passed unnoticed save for the fact that they were uttered by Couric (perhaps she and George were girlfriends). For the record, Couric tried to get Olivia Harrison to bawl as well, leaning in sympathetically and asking in her confide-in-me voice, "While he was sick [dramatic pause] how did he [longer dramatic pause] deal with that [pause] – the fact that there was something happening to his body, ravaging his body in fact, that he really couldn't control?"

Olivia was not moved to tears. If anything, she seemed to be deep in thought, perhaps trying to recall how to form the secret hand signal that would release the hounds. I pictured Couric scampering through the English countryside, ravenous canines at her eight-hundred-dollar heels. A sensible person might ask, "How do I get these vicious beasts to stop chasing me?" Katie would consult her notes and enthuse: "George loved the way these dogs dismembered unwelcome intruders."

You'd think the prospect of having to endure the cruel, sinister eyeliner of Katie Couric, let alone a red-carpet dissing from Joan Rivers, would serve as sufficient incentive to cease and desist all attempts to secure even moderate celebrity. But the truth is that the pursuit of fame has become America's national pastime, supplanting baseball and, more recently, crack.

Even if you watched the first instalment of *The Bachelor*, you probably have no recollection of Cathy. After all, she was among the first to be eliminated from competition, and therefore was to most viewers just one of twenty-five participants in the reality show's traditional Tournament of Whores Parade. But her fleeting moment in the national spotlight is significant in terms of what it reveals. Let's follow it through from the beginning.

At some point, Cathy decides to apply to appear on this new reality series. And she makes it; she's one of the women who will compete for the affection of Alex Michel, the titular eligible male. During her time on the program, she is depicted getting plastered on margaritas, enthusiastically thwacking her own heinie while performing a cowboy-themed erotic dance, and, finally, elegantly passing out in the can. Sensing that Cathy may not be exactly what he's looking for in a life partner, Alex sends her packing, ending her run on international television – except, however, for the obligatory reunion special, during which the girls are afforded an hour of prime time to gab about the man who so cruelly rejected them. Naturally, Cathy uses this opportunity to draw America's attention to her rack, which has, in the time between her drunken yee-hawin' and the taping of the reunion, been surgically enhanced. "You fix your car. You fix your house. I fixed myself," she told host Chris Robinson while theatrically gesturing to her chestal region.

Cathy's willingness to make with the personal revelations by no means establishes her as unique. In Canada, there was a thirteen-part TV series that aired on a cable channel in 2001. It began with a shot of a tattooed man having a shower and talking about his affinity for sado-masochism. Or rather, talking about how best to talk about his affinity for sado-masochism. "I'm flummoxed," he said, "as to how the hell to explain this to you in some way that it doesn't come across like something like felonious assault."

He pondered, and as he pondered he shaved around his goatee, a task that he said reflected his desire not to irritate the tender thighs of his S&M partner. Later, when we saw him standing naked, drill in hand, constructing an elaborate instrument of torture on which to restrain and abuse his beloved honey-pie, this polite grooming gesture seemed comically incongruous. The man's name, we were told, is Fogg. Fogg continued: "I guess what it boils down to is, if you're behind closed doors with someone you love, or even respect a whole bunch – well, it's nobody else's business what you do really." At which point the film crew took heed of that profound advice, turned off the cameras, and headed back to the office. Kidding. They stuck around long enough to document Vancouver's intriguing world of fetish parties, dungeons, cross-dressing, masters and slaves.

They called the show *Kink*. Round about the time that Fogg prepared to clip a rather nasty-looking contraption to his own scrotum, I came up with a more suitable and edifying title: *Don't Watch This If You'd Rather Not See Some Guy Clip a Rather Nasty-Looking Contraption to His Own Scrotum.*

Fogg introduced us to Fanny, a mother of two who described her "level of activity" with Fogg as ranging from "breaking the skin, bloodsports, to sexual control, rape scenes." There were no fake names or obscured faces in *Kink*, except for all the fellows in leather hoods, and I'd venture that was less an attempt at anonymity than an occupational requirement. Fogg said of Fanny, "I'm going to tie her up and hurt her. Not harm her – catch that? Not harm her, hurt her. It comes down to caring. You're sharing a moment of joy." Fanny, misting up, nodded: "It's true. It's all about love. . . . How many men do you know who would get up in the middle of the night and outfit your piercing chair?"

Damn you, Fogg, making life tougher for the rest of us guys with your interminable chivalry! "How the hell can we show you what we do?" Fogg wondered at the start of *Kink*. Hey, in this day and age, simply press the record button on the video camera.

3. Cream of Nandrolone

Old-timers insist there actually was an era in which an emotional meltdown was a relatively private experience, a distressing event that involved only a person's close friends or his immediate family or, for an employee of the United States Postal Service, his trigger finger. Nowadays, people line up to audition for the opportunity to weepily reveal their desires, inadequacies, and perversions. Why waste deep, eloquent concerns about your relationship on your cupcake alone? Get your toned bod on *Temptation Island III* and you can share your skepticism – and your ragin' abs! – with eighteen million viewers.

Let's face it: in a world that's seen Jerry and Oprah and Montel and Maury transform afternoon TV into a public soapbox for protestations and a confessional for transgressions, that's seen countless sports and film stars whine about the burden of fame and dubiously lament their whoring and drug-gulping ways, that's seen an American president claim a vast conspiracy and later beg forgiveness for being lamely serviced in the workplace by a tubby intern, we all wear an immunity necklace of sorts when it comes to televised expressions of remorse and despair. They want to pull on our heartstrings, but we've come to suspect they're just pulling our legs.

There's now a template for public revelations and public apologies and public denials; the process is that systematic, that ingrained in the popular culture. If you were, say, an athlete heading over to Athens for the 2004 Summer Olympic Games, would you be at all surprised to open up your Welcome Kit and find the following video?

Hi, I'm Troy McClure! You might remember me from such athlete-in-distress videos as *So You Halted Tiger's Winning Streak . . . by Intentionally Shattering His Fibula With a Fairway Wood!* and *Oopsy! I Just Masterminded the Gangland-Style Killing of My Cheerleading Rival!*

I'm here to talk to you about testing positive for performance-enhancing substances at these Olympics. If you haven't already done so, don't worry – you will! Everyone in amateur athletics is popping pills or injecting drugs into their cabooses nowadays. It's all the rage, just like casual sex in the 1970s and regretting having had casual sex in the 1970s in the 1980s.

But getting caught doesn't necessarily mean the ruin of your career, or even your afternoon! Sit back, relax, enjoy a cool, refreshing stanozolol cocktail. Here's all you need to know about coping with the public revelation that you are a walloping dopehead.

First, the plausible denial. Memorize this helpful tip: Olympic officials are not stupid, just imperious and corrupt. I know what you're thinking – they gave the Games to Athens and right now you're sharing a wooden shed with two hurdlers from Chad and a cranky goat, but trust me on this: they're not stupid. It took them only a couple of decades of viewing countless glaring instances of conspicuous cheating before they began to detect "the pattern of denial."

As one official explained in Sydney: "Athletes always say, 'It's not possible,' followed by, 'There must be some mistake in the sample,' followed by, 'I must have got it from the toilet seat,' followed by, 'Here's a writ for twelve million dollars from my lawyer.'"

I think you know where I'm heading: file the writ before you mention the toilet seat, and you're pretty much home free. If the pattern doesn't fit, they must acquit!

From that point on, it's all about making sure you don't slip up. You'll still be under suspicion, so stay alert and avoid your usual routines, such as strolling into the athletes' commissary and requesting a heaping bowl of cream of Nandrolone. If someone inquires about your copious acne, tell them it's merely a side effect of the revolutionary new Caramilk diet. And for heaven's sake, don't let anyone take a gander at your prostate, which we both know has ballooned to the size of a softball since you went on the juice! Ouchie!

Whether you're a devoted 19-norandrostenediol enthusiast or prefer the 'roid-rage that can only be generated by 19-norandrostenedione, remember that a positive drug test at the Olympics need not be a career-threatening occurrence.

You can survive it. You will survive it. And you'll go on to compete to your full, drug-aided potential, do your country and local pharmacist proud, and depart for home in the knowledge that the only obstacle remaining in your ordeal is coping with potential difficulty in urinating, jaundice, hepatic cholestasis, liver tumours, changes in the mechanism of blood clotting, high blood pressure, increased facial and body hair, impotence, serious neurological problems, and, in a few lucky fellows, a lingering case of priapism – the state of having a persistent and painful erection. Yowza!

Now get out there and show 'em what you're made of!

4. A Chubby Man in a Pink Polka-Dot Suit

What's most amusing about the modern age of celebrity is how neither its pervasiveness nor its hallowed place in the American experience nor its hold on the national conversation has had any effect on the average person's ability to identify and understand the way in which public images are constructed and manipulated. Think back to the 2001 Grammy Awards, which featured a much-publicized duet between singer/homosexual Elton John and rapper/purported homophobe Eminem. I can only imagine the ranks of puzzled faces the following morning in classrooms across the continent. Impressionable youths, the monstrous gay-bashing lyrics of rapper Eminem indelibly scrawled in their binders and their memories, trying to determine what to make of their idol's post-song embrace of a chubby gay man in a pink polka-dot suit.

LITTLE JOHNNY: "I mean, geez, he got so damn close to that fag Elton John and he didn't even kill him."

LITTLE MIKEY: "Maybe it's part of a master plan so fags'll trust him and he can totally kill more of 'em at once."

Young 'uns, at least, could be forgiven for possessing sufficient reserves of naïveté to be duped into taking Eminem at his hate-drenched word. But what was the excuse of the freaking-out hordes of grown-ups? How can we still be so naive as to fail to recognize that Eminem is a canny businessman first, a talented showman second, and a loathsome vulgarian only because it's (a) swell for his business and (b) integral to his showmanship? If his raps about butchering homosexuals or sodomizing his own mother wouldn't have sold, he'd have rapped about what did, be it urging the overthrow of a government or lambasting the heinous inferiority of artificial sweeteners. But oh the fuss! It's as though we'd somehow forgotten that rebel posturing and iconoclastic tirades are, after falling in love and getting dumped, the primary staples of songwriting.

Of course, Eminem is not really a rebel, never was, despite what Grammy organizers and CBS execs and, of course, Eminem want us to believe. To the contrary: he's a member of the Rap Establishment (Motto: "Proudly Dissing Bitches Since 1985!"), slapping a fresh coat of lyrical paint on a creaky ol' shtick that his prolific producer, Dr. Dre, and others have been peddling for the better part of two decades. Eminem graphically described killing his wife, just as Dre's N.W.A.

gloated about offing cops. Frankly, Roger Daltrey sounds more sincere when, still tickin' at the age of ninety-seven, he croaks: "Hope I die before I get old."

Remember, Eminem defiantly rapped, "You think I give a damn about a Grammy?" It was meant as a rhetorical question, a boastful testament to his unblemished maverick cred. And then he showed up at the 2001 ceremony, won an award, and promptly took out a piece of paper from which to read. *He'd prepared a speech!*

Strangely enough, the quest for an authentic rebel at those Grammys would have required a journey outside the Staples Center in Los Angeles and along the majestic red carpet, to the position at which arriving celebs were obliged to encounter the caustic and abrasive Joan Rivers. Now, like you, I have long delighted in mocking the obtuse musings and banal queries of this award-show inquisitor. At the Oscars one year, I sat carpet-side with dozens of celebrity-spotting enthusiasts who derived most of their pleasure from watching scads of famous faces try to deke past Joan's post.

But Rivers can be refreshingly seditious. On that Grammy night, she told us that everyone in the music business sleeps around. She made a bawdy reference to Angelina Jolie's relationship with her brother. She asked questions that were downright bizarre ("What are you going to do when your breasts go south?"), prompting awkward and – in rare instances – candid replies from her startled guests. She got the fellas from 'NSync to admit they get sick of singing the same songs. And she advised the gals from Destiny's Child to keep the free dresses they get while their careers are hot, because they'll need something nice to wear when they're back to being nobodies. Rivers didn't get to chat with Eminem, but I'd wager she would have had the guts to ask: "Why do you rap about killing gays and raping women but never find the time to accomplish these tasks in person?" And perhaps a few more kids out there would have clued in and been able to provide the answer on their own: because the recording acoustics and fine-dining options are rather limited when you're doing eight to twelve in a prison cell.

Searching for Michael Jackson's Nose: Future Newspaper Headlines

KING OF POP DENIES VOODOO CLAIMS
Jackson Insists He Never Put Death Curse on Steven Spielberg
Tried Anti-Aging Spell on "Adorable" Emmanuel Lewis, Though

PRESLEY EXPERIENCES FULL-BODY SHUDDER
Lisa Marie Abruptly Recalls: "I Was, Like,
Married *to That Freak!"*
Re-enters Memory-Suppression Therapy

BUBBLES THE CHIMP SUES JACKSON
Via Gestures, Suggests King of Pop Touched Him
"Down There"
Also Claims He Wrote All of *Bad*, Most of *Dangerous*

JACKSON FATHERS ANOTHER CHILD
Local Psychotherapists Rejoice;
Clear Schedules for 2019 and Beyond
Infant Expected "to Make Us All Fucking Rich!"

SEARCH FOR MICHAEL JACKSON'S NOSE ENDS
Missing Body Part Discovered in Al Capone's Secret Vault
Geraldo: "I Thought It Was a Walnut"

JACKSON NOW OFFICIALLY TRANSLUCENT
Celebrates 58th Birthday by Allowing
Passage of Light Through Body
"Kids Think I'm E.T.," He Boasts

JACKSON DENIES PLASTIC SURGERY REPORTS
"It's Ridiculous!" Singer Complains
"Only a Small Part of Me Is Plastic.
Most Is a Durable Titanium Alloy!"

MICHAEL JACKSON AGAIN TOPS CHARTS
Bests LaToya to Remain No. 1 on List of "Freakiest" Jacksons
Cites Disturbing Parenting Style, "Creepy" Visage for Success

MICHAEL JACKSON TURNS 65
"Nutty Child-Lovin' Pervert" Now Officially a "Dirty Old Man"
Entitled to 10% Seniors' Discount on All Child-Fondling Settlements

ELDERLY JACKSON GOES ON SHOPPING SPREE
Buys Several Rare Egyptian Antiquities, 17 Artificial Hips
Grateful Shopkeeper Ignores Fact Jackson Pantless

JACKSON SENILITY FEARED
When Signing Autographs, Identifies Self as "Matlock"
Staff Says He Spends Days in Kitchen
Trying to Clone Macaulay Culkin

JACKSON "CRYOGENICALLY" FROZEN
Staff Members Insist It Was His Dying Wish
Police Suspect Disgruntled Employees May
Just Have Locked Him in Freezer

THE BARBARA WALTERS INTERVIEW:
BARBARA WALTERS

BARBARA WALTERS: Good evening. Tonight, we turn the tables on one of the most distinguished interviewers of the modern era. For decades now, she has been the hunter, tracking and cornering the most desirable celebrity prey, merciless in her quest for personal confessions, for juicy revelations, and above all else for tears. She has made some of the famous people in America cry, and that in turn has made her one of the famous people in America. Tonight, however, the hunter becomes the hunted. With fascinating results.

BARBARA: Tell me about your childhood.

BARBARA: Listen, I know your tricks, Barbara. I'm not going to cry.

A crew member covertly zaps Barbara with a cattle prod.

BARBARA: Bwaaaaaaaah!

BARBARA(*smugly*): You were saying?

BARBARA (*wiping away tears*): Meg Ryan said that thing was painful, but I had no idea.

WHAT'S ON TV TONIGHT

	8:00	8:30	9:00	9:30	10:00	10:30
ABC	America's Blurriest Home Videos		According to John's Less Talented Brother	Whose Turn Is It to Do the Same Stupid Gag for the 800th Time Anyway?	Are You Pathetic? The Search for the Seven People Who Watched Are You Hot? The Search for America's Sexiest People	
CBS	Survivor: Jeff Probst's Rumpus Room		Further Evidence of Our Creative Bankruptcy (R)		Touched by a Charlie's Angel (Viewer Discretion Advised)	
NBC	Just Shoot Will & Grace	Already-Cancelled Sitcom	Law & Order: Really, Really Pushing Our Luck With the Law & Orders		Law & Order	
Fox	Live Humans Jabbed With White-Hot Spears	Stupid Morons Acting Like Complete Idiots	When Network Executives Attack!		Who Wants to Marry a Celebrity Boxer?	
CBC	You Paid for This Crud!		Fiddlin' With Fiddley MacFiddler	Toothless Satire	The Heroic Misadventures of Gwynne Dyer's Leather Jacket	
CTV	Obligatory Cancon Atrocity	Whatever the Americans Zap Up on the Satellite	That Stupid CTV Bouncing-Ball Promo Gets Its Own Show	Um, There's More Coming on the Satellite, Right? RIGHT?	Degrassi: Deep Space Nine	
Star!	The Making of the Making of Some Crappy Movie		The 25 Most Beautiful People in Show Business Whose Publicists Were Willing to Sleep With Our Producers		Celebrity Pocket Lint!	Madonna: Genius or Genius!
Showcase	Impatiently Awaiting the Funny Bits		Impatiently Awaiting the Car Chase		Impatiently Awaiting the Gratuitous Nude Sex Scene	

WHAT'S ON TV TONIGHT

	8:00	8:30	9:00	9:30	10 p.m.	10:30
TSN	Canada's Huskiest Dartsman		World Cup of Ice Fishing		Feeble Mimicry of ESPN Banter	
Food Network	Eat Up, Fatty!		Corpulent Sally	The Perspiring, Morbidly Obese Chef	It'll Turn Out Way Worse When You Try It at Home	
Animal Planet	The Crocodile Hunter		The Best of The Crocodile Hunter		The Crocodile Hunter Goes Grocery Shopping and Then Maybe to the Dentist or Something	
Lone Star	A Pleasure to Meet Ya, Miss Katie		I Reckon I Do, Zeke		Giddyup!	
CPAC	Blustery Twaddle	Twaddley Bluster	Caller? Are You There, Caller? I Think We've Lost the Caller		Asleep or Awake?: MPs During Commons Debates	
Fashion TV	Naked Boobs	Naked Butts	Naked Boobs & Naked Butts	Naked Butts & Naked Boobs	Annals of Photography: The Human Crotch	
W	I'm a Lesbian, Dammit!	My Bra, Myself	Empowerment Through Incessant Nagging		Unsubtle Moral Conveyed via Tedious Plotline	
Space	Robocrap		Planet of the Rudimentary Special Effects and Papier-Mâché Boulders		Star Trek: The Undiscovered Hairpiece	
A&E	Biography: The Only Celebrity Who's Yet to Be on Biography		Biography: The Guy Who Came Up With This Biography Idea		Biography: The Hot Girl Who Ignored the Biography Guy in High School but Now Totally Regrets It	

STAR TREK:
A CELEBRITY ITSELF

A man dressed as Spock departs his comic-book shop on his scooter at 11:14 a.m., heading due west towards the Star Trek convention at twenty-two kilometres per hour. At the same moment thirty kilometres across town, a jobless man done up as a Romulan exits an arcade and proceeds due east in his mother's Gremlin at forty-seven kilometres per hour.

At precisely what time does it become painfully obvious that neither of these guys is going to get laid today?

Star Trek depicts a utopian future, a future in which humanity has eliminated the scourges of racism and poverty – though, curiously, remains bedevilled by the more resilient scourge of unconvincing toupées. This follicular mystery notwithstanding, the original science-fiction television series, and the TV and film franchises that it spawned, ultimately attracted a large and loyal fan base. In a sense, the series itself became a celebrity, the subject of fawnfests and microscopic examination by enthusiasts who share a kinship with *Star Trek* characters, a deep affection for the ideals of their fictional universe, and, above all, a stated intention to move out of their parents' basement, like, ASAP. Seriously, they mean it this time.

For these Trekkers – true adherents reject the label "Trekkies," while many grudgingly accept such alternatives as "Trek nut" and "virgin" – *Star Trek* is more than an amusing pastime and reliable entertainment. It is a enviable template for our own society. In its depiction of a future in which humanity has banded together to solve societal problems and to explore the deepest regions of space, *Star Trek* imbues us with the hope that, if the people of Earth can learn to trust each other and work together towards a common purpose, there is no species in the galaxy that our starship captains cannot impregnate.

Star Trek shows us the way. It provides a set of values, a collection of deeply held beliefs. Some would even go so far as to say that *Star Trek* offers the fundamental framework of a viable religion, although these people would later admit that they had gotten carried away and immediately regretted even making such a ridiculous claim, and that it was probably the two glasses of chocolate milk talking.

This much, according to Trekkers, is certain: the manner in which the crew of the *Enterprise* – and in particular its captain – conducts itself should serve as a lasting lesson to us all. In times of crisis, when confronted with difficult decisions, even when all seems lost, we could do worse than to ask ourselves: What Would Kirk Do?

So, what would Kirk do?

Case Study: The Iraq Crisis of 2003

Situation: The world stands at the brink of war. U.S. President George W. Bush is threatening to invade Iraq and depose its president, Saddam Hussein, unless he is convinced that Iraq has turned over and disposed of all its weapons of mass destruction.

The video phone rings in the Grand Imperial Palace of Baghdad.
KIRK: This is Captain James T. Kirk of the Starship *Enterprise*. We come in peace.
SADDAM: Damn telemarketers. [*Muttering to self*] How the hell do you set up call blocking on this thing?
KIRK: No, hold on! I'm not selling anything. My people and I have travelled a great distance to deliver a message of friendship and unity.
SADDAM: Listen, you're tying up the line. I need to keep it clear for Hans Blix. [*Mimicking Blix's voice*] Saddam, we need to inspect this palace, that palace, every palace. Saddam, we're out of Heineken in the minibar.
KIRK: Just hear me out, Mr. President. Just hear me out.
Eight minutes later . . .
SADDAM: You make a convincing case, Kirk. Perhaps I should dispose of my weapons of mass destruction and embrace the –
A woman walks behind Saddam.
KIRK (*interrupting*): Whoa! Who's that absolutely divine creature in the background there, over by the bed?
SADDAM: What? Oh, that's just one of my wives.

KIRK: *One* of your wives?

SADDAM: Yes, I have several. But back to this intriguing matter of an earthly paradise that could be forged from –

KIRK: Don't they get jealous of each other? You know, cat fights? Girl-on-girl action. [*Making claws with his fingers*] Rrroaaw!

SADDAM: This hardly seems the time to discuss this. But no, there is no jealousy [*pause*] except maybe with regard to my harem of mistresses. Now when you speak of this magnificent Eden that we – [*Kirk has vanished from the video screen*] Hello? Hello? [*Smacks the video phone*] Blasted thing: I mean, sure, I saved money in the short term buying a Casio, but look – [*Kirk suddenly appears at Saddam's side. The Iraqi president is startled*] How the –

KIRK (*eyeing Saddam's lady friends*): I beamed down.

SADDAM: You defied the laws of physics to help me dismantle my sinister arsenal and willingly surrender my magnificent kingdom in the name of peace and global prosperity?

KIRK (*removing his shirt with a manly leer*): What? And give up the harem? Don't be so hasty there, compadre. There'll be plenty of time to usher in centuries of collective affluence and human well-being. [*Embraces the most copiously endowed of the assembled vixens*] But first, I need to personally inspect these weapons of mass stimulation.

Saddam looks on, bored. He gets up.

SADDAM: I'm going to go nuke Tel Aviv.

KIRK: Rrroaaw!

Analysis: Did Kirk protect the world from nuclear and biological peril and bring about the physical and spiritual advancement of the human species? Well, no. But he did get himself some lovin'. And when you're a Trekker, that is the true final frontier.

7:00 a.m. *Philoso-bots.* A thought-provoking program for children in which a league of super-philosophers uses contemplative reasoning, lexical ingenuity, and, if stuck in a really tight spot, an old-fashioned booty-whupping to make the world safe for Epistemological Relativism. Today: The Philoso-bots, led by the mighty Sock!rates, face their greatest challenge yet when they confront the biblical rhetoric and crushing kung fu grip of the medieval adherents of Divine Illumination.

8:00 *Pearls of Wisdom.* Roving camera crews visit locations around the world to ask citizens to share their deepest and most profound thoughts and sayings. From Beijing: "Time is the healer of wounds." From Paris: "Disobedience is the father of disrespect." From Hollywood: A series of helpful tips on how to distinguish surgically enhanced breasts from authentic ones.

10:00 *Celebrity Price Is Right.* Sure, Marx insists that goods should be distributed on the basis of need rather than endeavour. But will the revolutionary thinker actually surrender dibs on that Hawaiian-vacation showcase?

11:00 *Martha Stewart's Better Elitism.* Join Martha and guest Samuel Clemens as they craft a stylish yet functional homemade pipe from the bleached skull of a tuft-eared squirrel. Later, Martha enlivens the wardrobe of brainy economist

John Kenneth Galbraith by adorning his tweed jacket with elbow patches fashioned from delightful pea-green gingham.

12:30 p.m. *Health Break*. Today: How men can prevent the persistent rash that results from rubbing one's chin while deep in contemplative thought.

1:00 *Wisdom for Dummies*. A show designed to help people who have reached old age and yet, contrary to the societal expectation that they will have amassed substantial intellectual enrichment, are in fact more clueless about it all than ever. Regular features include Vague Answers to Pesky Queries About Mortality and, thanks to our ability to decode satellite feeds, the ever-popular listing of all the correct replies to tonight's episode of *Jeopardy!* Impress the whole family!

3:00 *Confucius Say: Welcome to My Writers' Workshop*. Join China's most famous teacher as he reveals the secrets of crafting precise treatises based on profound notions of humanism. Next week: How to cope with the emotional devastation of discovering 2,500 years later that your meditative observations are being mass-produced and stuffed into gimmicky, ill-tasting, after-dinner confections.

4:30 *Daily Comedy Break*. Being a cultural elitist doesn't necessarily mean you have to be a dour old puss! Oh, wait, yes it does. But get ready to laugh anyway as our very own Wisecracking Players ask the thigh-slapping question: Does language get in the way of self-knowledge?

5:00 *Fashion for the Male Cultural Elitist*. Today: How to wear an ascot without everyone immediately assuming you're gay.

6:00 *The Cultural Elitist News.* The events of the day, presented by an enlightened scholar who, after reading each item, either tut-tuts, makes a wry crack about history repeating itself, or sombrely laments, "I say, will these halfwits never learn?"

7:00 *Sanford and Son* (R).

7:30 *What Is the Meaning of Life?* Part 874 of our investigation into the purpose of our collective existence. Tonight: Our panel of profound thinkers endeavours to rule out the slim possibility that it's the pursuit of really comfortable underwear.

9:30 *Biography: The Three Wise Men.* A chronicle of their lives before that fateful trek across the desert, and a detailed re-enactment of the acrimonious debate over who'd get stuck with the myrrh.

11:30 *Late Night With Noam Chomsky.* Twelve minutes of commercials. Forty-eight minutes of Noam staring into the camera and begging you to not watch his show because it's a diversionary tool of a sinister mass media bent on protecting the minority of the opulent against a majority that they treat as ignorant and meddlesome outsiders. Tonight's guest: Lambchop.

12:30 a.m. *Sagaciously Reflective with Bill Maher.* Join Bill and his four guests – Aristotle, Nietzsche, Schopenhauer, and Jimmie "Dy-no-mite!" Walker – as they sit silently, stare intently into the distance, and mull tonight's topic: Why?

2:00 *Dead Air.* Or is it? Ponder.

A Two – Two, ah! ah! ah! – Two-Faced Snake

PRODUCER: Hey. Excuse me, you, with the feathers. Listen, we're from A&E. We're here to shoot some footage for a *Biography* special on Elmo. You know him?

BIG BIRD (*sipping a latte*): Sure, I know Elmo. Everyone on Sesame Street knows Elmo.

PRODUCER: Great. That's great. Let us just get the camera set up here and we'll ask you a few questions. Stories, anecdotes, fond memories – whatever you can come up with.

BIG BIRD: Oh, you don't want to talk to me. Elmo and I used to be good pals, but he doesn't hang out on the street much any more. I hardly ever see him these days.

PRODUCER: So talk about old times, when Elmo was first getting to be famous. [*To camera operator*] You ready? Okay, shoot.

BIG BIRD: All right. Well, that was when it all started to change, really. Elmo had always been a sweet little guy, even when he was starting to make it big. But then one year Bob McGrath took him to the Grammys, and Elmo was never the same.

PRODUCER: Got a bit of a big head, did he?

BIG BIRD: Well, not exactly. I think what happened is that at one of the after-parties, Bob introduced Elmo to P. Diddy, and they just hit it off. Dancing, laughing, partying. One minute Elmo's learning his alphabet and practising his phonics, the next he's chugging Cristal and calling Maria his "bee-yatch."

PRODUCER: Cut. That's great, Bird, great. But we're working more from the Elmo-is-adored-by-children-around-the-world angle.

BIG BIRD: Oh sure, he's all tee-hee-hee for the cameras. But yell "Cut!" these days and the kid's got a voice like Harvey Fierstein and a temper like Sean Penn.

PRODUCER: Right. [*Sees someone else coming*] Okay, thanks, Bird. Hey! Hey, blue guy. Over here. How about you? What do you make of Elmo's remarkable success?

COOKIE MONSTER: Me no want to talk about him.

PRODUCER: Come on, our viewers would appreciate it.

COOKIE MONSTER: Me say this. Me used to get all best cookies, real gourmet product. Now, budget all go to Elmo. Big trailer, masseuse, guest directors for his segments. Quentin Tarantino take forty-seven days to shoot balls-falling-out-of-closet gag. And then they make me do sketch with frickin' Dutch windmill cookies. Dutch windmill cookies. [*Pause*] Dutch. Windmill. Cookies.

PRODUCER: Er, right . . . You two! Stop! What about you two fellows? What can you tell us about Elmo?

ERNIE: Well, I don't know what you've heard, but he's a good kid.

PRODUCER: Finally! Get the camera over here.

ERNIE: A lot of folks on Sesame Street are jealous, though. I mean, a guy like Grover has been paying his dues for decades –

never bellyaching, not even when they stuffed him into a white disco suit for the cover of the *Sesame Street Fever* album – and he gets jack-all in the way of respect around here. But Elmo giggles and moults for fifteen minutes every day and he's got Emmys out the wazoo. It gets a little hard to take. Just yesterday, he shows up late for our rhyming-game segment. Eyes as red as his fur. And I'm not even going to tell you how he replied when I started the sketch by saying, "Pucker."

BERT (*nudging his way in*): You know at the end of the show, there's that bit where they say, "*Sesame Street* is brought to you by the letter F and the number five," or something like that. Well, Elmo has a hissy fit one day – storms off the set! – when the producers won't agree to change it to "*Sesame Street* is brought to you by Big Ol' Hank's Burger Hut and Tequila Bar." They always comp Elmo down at Big Ol' Hank's. The rest of us can't even run a friggin' tab.

PRODUCER: Cut. [*Sighs*] Burn that tape.

ERNIE: I hear that's why they gave him his own show a few years back – to keep him from bolting. Fox was after him to play the lead in a bawdy new sitcom opposite Tori Spelling and one of the California Raisins.

PRODUCER: Well, um . . . thanks. Cripes. [*Dejectedly*] How about you, sir? Do you have a minute to tell our viewers what you think of Elmo?

COUNT VON COUNT: Yes, I have precisely one – *one, ah! ah! ah!* – one minute to spare. So let me tell you a story, Mr. Producer Man. I run a little sideline business on Sesame Street: a public service involving financial repercussions resulting from the outcomes of certain events of a sporting nature, if you catch my drift. [*The producer stares ahead vacantly*] I'm a friggin' bookie. Anyway, Elmo gets on the show, starts earning a little green. Next thing I know he's knocking on my castle door. Kid got lucky at first, real lucky: he always bet that the baker guy with the cakes would wind up falling down those stairs. Clumsy oaf cost me a fortune! But then Elmo started wagering on hopscotch, on rock-paper-scissors – he was out of control, and his luck turned bad. Soon, the kid's into me for five – *five, ah! ah! ah!* – for five large. But every time I go to collect, I get a face-full of fat furry enforcer, telling me to scram. You ask me, the kid's a two – *two, ah! ah! ah!* – two-faced snake.

There is a pause.

PRODUCER: Screw this. Let's hit the road. I say we try something a little easier this afternoon, like getting Mia Farrow to say some nice things for the Woody Allen bio.

As the producer and his crew depart, they walk past the Sesame Street Four Seasons, where Elmo is in the hot tub shooting a segment for his show, Elmo's World.

ELMO (*wearing sunglasses and nursing a highball while bikinied Muppets peel grapes for him*): Hi, kids! Elmo loves you! Today we're going to learn all about "groupies."

Materiel Girl

In the spring of 2003, the United States and the United Kingdom were at war with Iraq when word came that Madonna was poised to release a war-themed video to promote her new song, "American Life." A nation pronounced itself relieved – relieved that a bona fide music superstar was finally poised to tell them what to think of the military assault on this despotic regime. But only hours before the video's North American premiere, Madonna decided to scrap its release, decreeing that she did "not want to risk offending anyone who might misinterpret the meaning of this video."

Typical celebrity behaviour. Very selfish. A profoundly important global event was underway in the Middle East and here we were, half a world away, left without a Madonna-endorsed point of view. Like the rest of you, I have long looked to the Material Middle-Aged Woman and other top-selling musical performers for guidance on the opinions I should hold (even now, I'm still waiting to see if Britney comes out for or against shingles) and the behaviour I should exhibit, and it's always worked out pretty well, except for the days following the release of "Like a Prayer." Local law-enforcement officials never did accept Madonna's video as an excuse for my erecting all those crosses on my front lawn and setting them ablaze.

Luckily, Madonna has taught us all to be dogged and persistent ("Papa Don't Preach," 1986). Deprived of access to her new video, I instead scoured for hints about her views on military conflict among the many thoughtful and edifying videos this respected commentator on global affairs has produced during the past two decades.

Like a Virgin

PLOT: Dolled up like a two-dollar tramp, Madonna stretches and splays herself into an array of trollopy poses while travelling through Venice in a gondola.

INTERPRETATION: Whores tend to be in favour of wars, what with them being excellent for business and all.

CONCLUSION: Madonna supported the military conflict in Iraq.

Open Your Heart

PLOT: Madonna gamely displays her bounteous cleavage to the lustful patrons of a peep show, then skips off into the distance with a horny young boy.

INTERPRETATION: Madonna's stripper represents wise and peace-minded political leadership. The horny young boy represents the world's innocence. In the end, the two get together, which suggests Madonna believes it is peace-minded leaders who will protect the world's innocence. Or, possibly, that she believes in personally tending to the sexual needs of the world's horny young boys.

CONCLUSION: Madonna opposed the military conflict in Iraq.

Cherish

PLOT: Madonna frolics playfully on a beach, gets all wet and sexy, and bends over a lot so we can stare at her ass.

INTERPRETATION: This particular beach is not being stormed heroically by D-Day soldiers. At least that's my recollection. I can't be too sure because I was mostly staring at Madonna's ass.

CONCLUSION: Madonna's ass opposed the military conflict in Iraq.

Express Yourself

PLOT: Madonna angrily dances about while wearing a cone-shaped bra that bears a rather pointed resemblance to the tip of a missile.

INTERPRETATION: Madonna is cagily referencing and, with just a precious dollop of her singular feminist whimsy, deriding the inherent sexual subtext of all military confrontations. Either that, or she's saying her breasts are capable of killing scores of innocent civilians and must therefore remain securely harnessed at all costs.

CONCLUSION: Madonna opposed the military conflict in Iraq, but remains very much in favour of her bosom.

Justify My Love

PLOT: Madonna, attired in a raincoat and immodest lingerie, strolls through the halls of a hotel in Paris. Then she has sex with a porn star.

INTERPRETATION: Paris is in France.

CONCLUSION: Madonna opposed the military conflict in Iraq. Also, she's willing to boff pretty much anyone.

So there we have it. The preponderance of evidence available in past videos suggests that Madonna opposed the military conflict in Iraq, and therefore so did I. Bad war! Bad, bad war! Now excuse me: I've got to tune into Black Entertainment Television to see if I'm for or against black women who frenetically shake their rumps while being ogled by wealthy hip-hop stars.

Ways to Make Hockey
More Popular Among Television
Viewers in the United States

✔ All players with foreign-sounding, European-type names such as Jaromir and Pavel henceforth to be referred to as "Justin Timberlake."

✔ At the end of each period, players required to cast ballots to expel a teammate from the game.

✔ New rule for goaltenders: Make a save, chug a beer.

✔ To assist U.S. marketing efforts, one player on each club must legally change name to Wayne Gretzky.

✔ Two Zambonis drive onto ice at intermission – only one comes off!

✔ To heighten appeal of sport among American youth, league's next expansion franchise to be awarded to J.Lo.

✔ Stanley Cup Finals officially renamed Stanley Cup Smackdown.

✔ Standard post-goal embrace replaced by choreographed dance number featuring Rob Lowe and Snow White.

✔ Dressing-room footage enhanced by Smell-o-Vision!

✔ Game-dulling "trap" negated by expertly placed landmines in neutral zone.

✔ Old slogan: The Coolest Game on Earth! New slogan: Almost Always Less Boring than Soccer!

For all the good it has done, for all the information it conveys, the Internet remains primarily a diabolical medium, tacitly encouraging otherwise sentient individuals to believe that the world longs to see the digital photographs of their family vacation to Delaware. In the minds of many, the World Wide Web has democratized the notion of celebrity. Madonna has a home page; you have a home page. Ergo, you = Madonna. Except you ≠ Madonna. You = the family that went to Delaware. The urge to carve celebrity from anonymity is the new national obsession, played all year round in front of a computer screen.

Hey, y'all, and welcome to my, like, online journal and all. So you want to know what it's like to be an offensive lineman at training camp in the National Football League? Well, let me tell you, it is a lot of hard, hard work – and that's just finding an athletic cup that fits me! Ho, ho, ho. Seriously though, here is my diary from yesterday so you can see for yourself!

6:30 a.m. Wake-up call. Waited patiently for the team "crane" to arrive to help me out of bed. That's just a figure of speech, by the way: "Crane." It's not really a crane – it's more like a team of four stout men operating an integrated series of ropes and pulleys crafted onto a mechanism forged from an unbreakable titanium alloy. But the veterans call it a crane. Those guys will take any opportunity to razz a rookie like me!

7:00 Mandatory steroid test. Tried to remember which glass in the fridge was the "clean" urine I purchased from that kid at Burger King and which was my leftover pineapple smoothie. I thought I got it right, but then heard later from the lab that I'd tested positive for artificial fruit flavouring.

7:30 Breakfast. Two eggs, a bagel, and four strips of bacon. Oops, my roommate Peyton just told me that those things I ate weren't bacon "strips" but rather bacon "slabs." What's that, Peyton? Six-pound slabs? Thanks, buddy! (That Peyton sure is helpful. And what a joker! My first day at camp he comes up to me and he hollers, "God almighty, are you ever one big honkin' fat fatso!" All the other guys laughed, so I did, too. Later, I heard him bet some other fella "five large" that I'd be dead of heart failure before I'm twenty-five. I'd never have guessed Peyton was such a comedian!)

8:30 Morning practice. It's always nice to get out on the field before it gets too hot! Although technically I wasn't actually on the field this morning – I was out working on a "secret pattern" given to me by Coach himself! He said he picked me special on account of my "unique attributes." Anyway, I did what he said and ended up telling some writer (I mean, the guy didn't look like a writer to me, but Coach insisted he's a "bookie") that Coach ain't going to be paying him nothing that he owes him. Seemed to be a lot of money in question: I didn't know Coach was such a lover of literature! Anyway, you're probably wondering how this "secret pattern" is going to help me on the field. I do, too, but who am I to question Coach?

10:15 Practice over. After undressing, I was lucky to catch a glimpse of myself in the mirror of the trainers' room, so I took the opportunity to silently wish my annual greeting to my penis. Nice to see you again, little guy!

10:30 Meetings. There sure are a lot of meetings at training camp! It's almost like being back in college again, except this time there aren't any alumni to force some brainiac geek to go in your place. ;-) But we do learn a lot of important stuff, like how to protect against a safety blitz and which skanky groupies not to have intercourse with during away games in Buffalo. (Candy, if you're reading this: You really ought to take better care of *you*.)

12:00 p.m. Lunch. The veterans have this prank where they get up and walk away from the table when I sit down. Hilarious! But it was probably for the best today, or otherwise I'd never have been able to fit that whole entire pig on the table.

1:30 Hey, wow! I've hit the big time, y'all! My mom just called to tell me that someone's selling one of my practice jerseys on eBay. If you want to bid on it, just follow the links. Click on this category: Tents (Sleeps Four).

2:00 Afternoon practice. My big chance! Coach puts me in with the first-stringers, so I'll actually be protecting Peyton, our quarterback! I'm not going to lie to you: I was a little bit nervous, which may help to explain why I tripped and fell when I got to the huddle. Yeah, it could have been Peyton's outstretched foot, too, I guess. But that doesn't make me feel any better about knocking Peyton over as I fell and then landing on his head.

3:30 Autograph session. Don't nobody know who I am – yet!! – so I just hang out and watch Peyton sign. It's weird, though: he's got this kind of far-off look in his eye, and he's drooling a lot, and instead of writing his name he keeps signing "Jackie Collins" or "Love, Grandma." Then the trainer comes over and asks Peyton how many fingers he's holding up, and Peyton says: "Eleventy-eight." That Peyton – he's hilarious!

4:15 Chilled in the whirlpool for a bit, and noticed that some of the veterans were starting to call me "USS *Preble*." That confused me a bit at first, but then Coach told me the *Preble* is a guided-missile destroyer that has a displacement of 9,217 tons. Coach says that's the exact same as me, which I guess is a compliment, right?

5:30 Dinner. Want to look and smell my best after a hard day on the field, so I grab a shower and crack open a new bottle of Calvin Klein's Futility for Men. Got a whole case of the stuff when I got drafted by the Cincinnati Bengals!

7:00 Relax by playing a little Madden with some pals. Gotta tell ya, I don't like this new version, the one they put out after agreeing to reduce the amount of violence in the game. I mean, I just sent Ray Lewis up the middle on a blitz to sack the quarterback – and then Lewis celebrated by pouring himself a glass of sherry and remarking drolly on the state of the global economy. Call me crazy, but I prefer the old-fashioned ritualistic beheadings.

8:00 Study time. Coach wants us to hit the books. :-(After practice, he did this funny thing where he went into his office and came out with a book of *Beetle Bailey* cartoons that he gave to me "on account of the fact you can't read worth a shit, Preble." But the joke's on Coach because I can read plenty good, right, Gerry? (Gerry is the guy who's typing all this into his computer because I can't spell.)

9:20 Oh, Sarge, will you ever win?

9:45 Sneaking in a little TV before bedtime, and I see this car commercial with what's-her-nose . . . Celine Dion. I'd heard nasty things about her, but she didn't seem all that bad to me. I mean, her hair was done up so nice you could hardly see the horns or pointed ears.

10:00 Lights out. My roommate Peyton is always thinking of me and helping me out. He says I need my sleep, so tonight he gave me this special "serenity sack" which I'm supposed to put over my head to get me some quality shut-eye. Looks like a regular plastic bag to me, but I'm just a rookie, so what do I know?

The Fin Thing Again

Notes for an oral presentation to an emergency session of the Federal Communications Commission in the United States.

Esteemed commissioners,

Let me begin by acknowledging that I am in the commission's debt – first, for convening this hearing on such short notice, and, second, for hastily installing this large aquarium in which I am now ensconced. And may I just add: Yummy molluscs! You folks are first class.

For those of you who don't know me from my previous appearances before this commission, or my now-legendary guest-starring role on the jump-the-shark episode of *Happy Days*, I am . . . a shark. My species doesn't descend to such mundane matters as conferring names on one another, but for purposes of identification let the record show that I have two small scars on my head – the unfortunate by-product of my memorable appearance in the hit motion picture *Austin Powers in Goldmember*. (*Pause for applause*) I still can't believe Myers wouldn't let me keep my frickin' laser. (*Pause for laughter*)

I appear before you today at the urgent behest of others of my kind, and indeed of the animal kingdom as a whole. If you'll open the briefing binders I've had prepared for you, and turn to Table 14f, you will find the prime-time programming schedules for Discovery Channel and Animal Planet. Allow me to read the titles of some of these programs: *Shark Chasers*; *Air Jaws II*; *3D Sharks*; *Shark Summer*; *Sharks: The Silent Killers*; *Shark Attack Files III* . . . (*gestures theatrically with pectoral fin to convey notion that list goes on*)

Honourable commissioners, as if I need to remind you, it's Shark Week again. And you may be tempted to ask: When is it not Shark Week these days? Good question, esteemed commissioners. Good question. This Shark Week business has been going on ever since the initial proliferation of specialty cable channels: the relentless persecution of my kind presented as "educational programming"; the wetsuited biologists shoving high-tech cameras into our deadened eyeballs; the electronic sensors and homing beacons and other glittery research gizmos they've left dangling from us, to the point that some of my best friends will, for the rest of their lives, look as though they're dolled up for a Mr. T look-alike contest. It's getting so a guy can't rip the spine from a defenceless elephant seal pup in privacy any more. Ladies and gentlemen of the FCC, I ask you. I ask your species. Do we bug you while you're at work?

It is my sad duty to report that Shark Week is only growing more repulsive and unconscionable. Recent instalments have featured not just the usual recreational prodding by (*uses pectoral fins to make air quotes*) "researchers," but also the gratuitous inclusion of (*uses same pectoral fins to make exaggerated air quotes*) "celebrities," such as David James Elliott, That Guy from the Band Sugar Ray, and Casper Van Dien. As if it's not bad enough that we have to endure the harsh TV lights and the vile, tasteless goop that these cheapo documentarians have the nerve to call chum, now our resilient species, which has plied the oceans for millions of years, is reduced to being the scenic back-drop to a paying gig for the dork from *Starship Troopers*?

The shame only deepens, alas. A recent shark-related program opened with several shots of the bikinied crotch of (*the fin thing again*) "Hollywood actress" Estella Warren frol-icking suggestively in a lagoon. Estella went on to showcase her nerve and, more frequently, her cleavage as she plunged into the water and "tickled the tummies" of passing sharks. Let us leave aside the confounding business of how your species can find attractive such a hideous creature – that flawless, creamy skin . . . *eww!* – and focus instead on the ignominy of it all, the objectification of my species and the fact that Discovery Channel hasn't even had the decency to respond to my request for a cut of the residuals.

For purposes of edification, I left a tape of this Estella Warren episode with the FCC research branch, and I was happy to hear that many of you on the commission took the opportunity to watch it. Several times, in some cases. So you will surely understand that I conclude my presentation this morning with a plea. As you deliberate future licences for broadcasting entities, we encourage you – *we beg you* – to consider the distress and the misery and the absurdly sombre narration that has been inflicted upon my kind. With the explosion of specialty television channels – across North

America and around the world – you humans don't have to tax your precious opposable thumb to find any number of programs about shark life, shark ways, shark attacks, shark secrets, and even shark procreation.

And you people have the nerve to say *we're* the ones prone to feeding frenzies.

WHAT A CROC!

Nature programs used to be the domain of the telephoto lens and the solemn narrator, of prolonged sequences of industrious bark-gnawing, the reverential voice-over falling silent for minutes at a time to permit viewers to take in the ambient soundscape. Nowadays, it's all about which khaki-clad yokel can come closest to having his nuts chomped off by an ornery reptile. Had he been on television today, Marlin Perkins would have been forced to narrate *Mutual of Omaha's Wild Kingdom* while standing knee-deep in the Everglades, his octogenarian rump encased in a stylish loincloth, his mind strategically pondering the potential ratings windfall of sacrificing his loyal assistant Jim to a famished alligator.

The reigning king of the modern televised jungle is Steve Irwin, better known as the Crocodile Hunter, best known as the Human Exclamation Mark. Although there are countless species of animal upon this planet, and although nature is a resolutely unpredictable force, damn near every encounter between the Crocodile Hunter and an exotic creature goes exactly like this: Discovery of creature. Grabbing and hoisting of creature. Immediate utterance of one to three catchphrases ("By crikey, this beauty's a naughty girl!") Prodding. More prodding. Expression of seemingly genuine surprise that creature suddenly seems irritated and aggressive. Yet more prodding, squeezing, yanking, molesting. Attempt by exasperated creature to bite, sting, or otherwise maim this annoying Australian freak. Utterance of any remaining catch-phrases not yet uttered. Expression of tender affection for creature. Gentle stroking of creature. Disturbing cooing to creature. Planting of kiss full on the mouth of creature. Dropping of creature and sprinting off-camera.

The Crocodile Hunter has long been billed as a program that promotes the understanding of exotic species, but the truth is that it mostly promotes Steve Irwin. It is he, not the critters, who is the star of the show, and viewers – especially young men, who form the reliable core of the audience – are generally attracted to the proceedings not by the prospect of learning about wetlands conservation but rather by the prospect of that ridiculous Australian chap losing his manhood to a cranky croc. Attempting to deconstruct such an inexplicable phenomenon could consume the academic life of a Ph.D. candidate, or at the very least one full sentence in a book: He acts as though he's eight years old.

That seems to be the show's defining element, Irwin's juvenile abandon. He dresses like a kid, flops to the ground and gestures wildly like a kid. He talks with the exaggerated cadence and limited vocabulary of a kid. He even moves like a kid: his shoulders rolling, his chest thrust out, his gait awkward yet urgent. He stumbles onto a snake or a scorpion and you can't help but think he's going to carry it home and beg his mommy to let him keep it. Irwin's persona is so finely crafted, so seamless in its presentation, that it becomes impossible even to fathom what he might be like on the rare occasions when he is not being sprayed with snake venom or stalked by lions or bending down to slap a loving embrace on a lethargic pregnant croc. One can only imagine a typical household encounter with his wife, Terri:

TERRI: Uh, Steve, could you please pass the ketchup?
STEVE (*hoists ketchup and commences shaking it roughly*): Crikey! Isn't this bottle of ketchup a beauty? (*Eyes bulge out*) It's gorgeous! Whoa, you're going to spill all over me and stain my short pants, aren't you, you naughty ketchup? Naughty bottle! Danger! Danger! There you go, girl. There you go. Woo-hoo!
TERRI: *Zzzz.*

Irwin has been compared to no small number of famous showmen and shtick artists, but the person he most reminds me of is Mary Hart. He approaches the animal kingdom with the same overbearing enthusiasm and unvarying fondness that Mary brings to her encounters with celebrities. The zeal with which he discusses the breeding habits of the Madagascar lemur, for example, is reminiscent of how Mary described Julia Roberts's wedding dress. Wow! Golly gee! Crikey!

And like Hart, Irwin has the rare, and not entirely enviable, ability to make something both more entertaining and much less interesting.

THE LARRY KING INTERVIEW:
E.T. THE EXTRA-TERRESTRIAL

LARRY: Good evening, ladies and gentlemen. What a treat we have for you tonight. Our first guest is the star of one of the greatest and most popular movies of our time. Of any time, really. Children, adults, even the smartest of our domestic pets – they all fell in love with him. More than two decades later, that love endures and is now being experienced by a whole new generation. He's here to take your phone calls. What a thrill. We welcome to the program E.T. The Extra-Terrestrial.

E.T.: Too kind, Larry. I'm blushing.

LARRY: Listen, before we begin, thanks for flying in. I mean it.

E.T.: Not a problem. I had a thing over at the Nike store anyway.

LARRY: Let's go back a bit. The film – your film, your big hit – it was re-released in theatres for its twentieth anniversary. Big publicity, a huge publicity machine behind it. And yet you didn't do the cast reunion show on TV. Why?

E.T.: It's all about respect, Larry. I mean, why should I join the group hug when I'm not getting shown any love?

LARRY: I'm not sure I understand.

E.T.: Everything I read in the trades, everything I saw on *Access Hollywood*, it's always Spielberg going on about how for years he'd wanted to "fix" certain elements of my performance. My eyebrow didn't arch right in one scene, or some garbage like that. I didn't produce a "credible" emotion or whatever. Even the way I sprinted wasn't good enough –

LARRY: Too smooth.

E.T.: Yeah, too smooth, that's what he'd say. So he goes and gets the CGI dweebs to give me a lope. *A lope!* I mean, here's a guy who cast Robin Williams in *Hook*, and he's obsessing over *my* performance?

LARRY: You're offended he tinkered with your work.

E.T.: Yeah, but I'm not surprised. He always referred to me as his "animatronic creature," like I was his big cuddly puppet or something. Steven likes to dehumanize.

LARRY: Kate Capshaw, Steven's wife, lovely lady. Good mother. Great actress. She's been on the program before.

E.T.: Um . . . okay.

LARRY: What do you make of Spielberg's decision to use computer-graphic imaging to remove guns from the hands of police officers and put walkie-talkies in their place?

E.T.: Funny story: that was actually my suggestion. Although I thought he should have replaced them with grenade launchers. Kids today are more savvy: they aren't impressed by anything less than a grenade launcher.

LARRY: You ever date Loni Anderson?

E.T.: That was a rumour, Larry. Someone saw me and Burt Reynolds in a fist fight and made the assumption. But I was just pissed at Burt for not casting me in *Cop and a Half*.

LARRY: When *E.T.* played in theatres, did you go to see the revised version?

E.T.: Yeah, I snuck into a screening. Sat at the back and watched how people reacted. Watched a whole new generation fall in love with the story. Watched how all of them laughed at the "penis breath" line, even though so few seemed to grasp the connotation. I mean, here's this ten-year-old boy who's basically accusing his brother of –

LARRY: Right. Fellatio. Great scene, but that always nagged at me.

E.T.: Me, too. And I don't even have genitalia.

LARRY: You know, frankly, I'm surprised you were able to enjoy the film in peace. It must have been quite a scene when people realized who you are. What kind of comments did you get?

E.T.: Pretty much same as always: "Hey, look, it's Mickey Rooney! Can I have your autograph, Mr. Rooney?" That sort of thing.

LARRY: Mickey, class act. Dated several of my ex-wives. [*Awkward silence*] You're a pro. You're a huge star. But we haven't seen a lot of you on the big screen lately.

E.T.: Well, that's Hollywood: One day you're on top of the world, the next you're dry cleaning your white suit and begging to replace Hervé Villechaize on *Fantasy Island*. And just between you and me, that really was a low point for Peter Coyote.

LARRY: He would have been good in that role. He's tall, but he can play short.

E.T.: But yeah, Larry, it was tough: I'd go to auditions and I'd get these looks, these looks that said, "Even if you give the greatest reading ever delivered in the history of cinema, there ain't no way we're signing you to play Drago in *Rocky IV*."

LARRY: Cruel business. Has it ever worked in your favour? Your . . . origins.

E.T.: Well, I actually got the lead in *Six Days, Seven Nights*. Anne Heche and I had done a vaudeville thing together back on her home planet, so we knew how to play off each other. But the studio ended up bringing in Harrison Ford and doing reshoots.

LARRY: Harrison Ford, great actor, good hair. Hair like a man's hair ought to be. [*Silence. Somewhere, a wolf howls*] But why did they lose confidence in you?

E.T.: Let's just say the response of the audience at the test screening – especially to the explicit love scene – was rather . . . profane.

LARRY: That old taboo: interspecies fornication . . .

E.T.: And yet when Harvey Keitel did it with Holly Hunter in *The Piano* . . . nothing!

LARRY: Say "E.T. phone home."

E.T.: No.

LARRY: Come on, say it. Say it just once.

E.T.: No way. Stop it.

LARRY: E.T. phone home!

E.T.: I knew I should have done this with Connie Chung.

LARRY: Coming up next, your phone calls for E.T. The Extra-Terrestrial. And later in the program: Today he was impeached by the Senate, this afternoon he resigned from office, and tonight he's our guest. The former president of the United States will be here to take your phone calls! Stay with us.

INTELLECTUAL PROPERTY

As a single tear descended his left cheek, streaming across the tattoo of a bloodied dagger before disappearing into his thick stubble, Emmitt "Slasher" McClelland choked back a sob and put it plainly: "We just can't take it any more."

Mr. McClelland, a thirty-six-year-old murderer, rapist, and fledgling extortionist, had just been elected the first president of the newly formed Brotherhood of Criminals, Fugitives, and Electrical Workers. The union represents about 13,800 scofflaws who perpetrate or abet felony-class criminal acts in the continental United States.

"I think I speak for all my brothers when I say, being a thug, a hood, even a henchman – it's stressful enough at the best of times. You're always thinking to yourself, Is the gun gonna go off accidentally when I shove it in my pants? Where am I gonna dump the next corpse? What if Sick Wally or Mickey the Perv beats me to the punch and starts stalking that hot new Laker Girl? It's tough on the nerves," Mr. McClelland told reporters who were covering the union's founding convention. "And now we got this to deal with too."

Mr. McClelland was referring to the ever-increasing demand from television cop shows for criminal acts that generate substantial and enduring media coverage, which in turn allows these offences to be "ripped from the headlines" and used as the basis for compelling, ratings-grabbing storylines on popular TV crime series. It was bad enough when it was just *Law & Order*, Mr. McClelland says; now there are three *Law & Orders*, two *CSIs*, and, for criminals, one unrelenting demand to feed the television beast.

"You see those promos on TV: 'This crime, ripped from the headlines. That crime, ripped from the headlines.' But you don't think about all the work and all the effort that goes into perpetrating those crimes. I mean, I'm a criminal, yes. But I'm also an artist, and I'm sick and tired of my work being exploited."

Mr. McClelland told reporters that neither he nor any of the union's members receive any royalties or creative recognition for their inspiring and typically homicidal endeavours. "All we get is the hassle," he lamented. "Producers calling us in the middle of the workday: 'We need more material!' I swear to God, if Dick Wolf sends me one more fruit basket, I'm personally gonna jam a papaya up his ass." Mr. McClelland paused to compose himself before continuing. "I want financial compensation, Mr. Wolf, not an associate-producer credit. And that's what this union is all about. I mean, this is our intellectual property and it's being stolen from us. But if I were to try to tell that to the cops, *I'm* the one who'd be arrested. It's crazy, just crazy."

Pressed by reporters, Mr. McClelland shared the details of his own recent traumatic experience involving a double homicide of which he was particularly proud. "I'd really put some thought into this one," he said, smiling. "You know, innovative use of unconventional weaponry, building in a couple of false leads, crafting a nice dramatic arc, that sort of thing. It made all the papers, front page, day after day. Sure enough, eight months later, I see it in the *TV Guide*. My crime. My crime on *Law & Order*. So I invite the gang to my place, I go to the trouble of knocking over a convenience store to make sure I've got beer and whatnot, and then I'm watching the show with my buddies and, fuck me, I see they changed the ending. The guy playing me not only gets collared, he gets sent away for life – *after breaking down in tears on the stand!* Now what kind of message does that send to the rookie criminal, the guy just starting out? It says, Don't bother being original. Don't bother going to the trouble of making the headlines. Because in the end we're just gonna demean you, disrespect you, make you look like a fool. I mean, here's an industry that needs us, that needs us to keep doing what we do. And they're treating us like we're the bad guys!"

While reducing the pressure from television networks for compelling storylines is far and away the top priority of Mr. McClelland's administration, there are other issues that need to be addressed. For instance, Mr. McClelland's campaign platform included a pledge to implement a system to regulate the granting and use of nicknames among American criminals. "It can get confusing," Mr. McClelland said matter-of-factly. "On the union executive alone, we've got three Slashers, three Shotguns – Shotgun Steve and, get this, two Shotgun Earls – and a pair of Twisted Petes. It's a nightmare just taking attendance."

FABULOUS!

Well, you need doctors. If you want to pitch a TV show that has even a hope of getting made, you pretty much need to have some doctors. Doctors are good. But not just any doctors. Have a look at the kind of doctors that are already on television: you need spunky, conflicted doctors who won't take no for an answer, dammit. If you're trying to devise the Perfect Pitch – the ideal confluence of dramatic and comedic elements that will result in your being hastily presented with a sweet development deal, untold financial riches, and, in all likelihood, a passionate French kiss from a powerful network boss in a twenty-five-hundred-dollar suit – those are the kind of doctors you need.

You also need criminals and cops. A lot of criminals. You need a lot of criminals perpetrating a lot of crimes, though not well enough that the crimes take any longer than an hour to solve. You need criminals who are clever enough to keep the cops guessing, but not so smart that they won't fess up after roughly four minutes of terse, theatrical interrogation. So you need doctors. You need criminals. And you need cops – preferably eccentric, renegade undercover cops who play by their own set of rules. Then, naturally, you must place them all in a modest single-family dwelling occupied by a lovable yet charmingly discordant blue-collar family.

So here's the pitch: An hour-long dramedy in which a lovable yet charmingly discordant blue-collar family transforms its modest living room into a medical clinic staffed by spunky, conflicted doctors who won't take no for an answer, dammit, and who in the course of not taking no for an answer cross the line and break the law and are then brought to justice by the members of the lovable yet charmingly discordant blue-collar family, who all along were, in fact, eccentric, renegade undercover cops who play by their own set of rules. Plus there's an abandoned puppy in there somewhere. It's not just any show – it's every show!

Months after making the Perfect Pitch, you may well find yourself in Hollywood, sitting on a stage and staring out at two hundred people who watch television professionally ("professionally," of course, being the fancy word for "whilst wearing one's underpants"). Each March, professional baseball players gather down south to prepare for the season ahead. It's a rather fitting rite of spring, what with its bucolic ambience, its connotation of rebirth, and its suggestion of the seemingly infinite possibilities of a fresh start. Similarly, each July, television critics gather out west to prepare for the coming season of U.S. network television. It's a rather fitting rite of summer, what with its overheated rhetoric, its ability to generate sweat (most notably upon the brow of any executive who alleges the inherent comic rapture of Bob Saget's latest show), and its suggestion that prolonged exposure to an object – the sun, for instance, or the pilot for anything starring Brooke Shields – will result in pronounced agony.

It's known as the Press Tour, an event that draws not only the major American broadcast networks, but also the astonishing bevy of cable broadcasters, including Nickelodeon, Animal Planet, Hallmark Channel, and Oxygen. There has been an explosion of viewing options in the past few years, yet ratings indicate people are spending less time in front of the television, a statistical curiosity that can probably be explained by the fact that so many people are making TV programs these days that there's hardly anyone left to watch them. Still, hope springs eternal in Hollywood, blending with the copious reserves of insincerity and pretension to fashion a mighty gusher of counterfeit effervescence, which serves as the lifeblood of the ruthlessly cheery publicists and ruthlessly ruthless executives of American television. The result is this two-week dog-and-pony show, during which the cable channels and the networks insist their dogs are ponies and their ponies are thoroughbreds. To which the assembled TV scribes routinely mutter, "Neigh."

The faces change every year (actually, it's mostly the same actors and executives; their faces, however, have been tucked, ripped, and sculpted) but the fundamentals remain the same: during the Press Tour, critics gather to hear about the new TV season, talk with performers and producers, and fiercely debate such seminal questions as "Is the medium of television in an inexorable moral decline?" and, somewhat more frequently, "Do you think her knockers are real, or what?" It's an event that could not possibly exist if anyone involved dared to utter a word of truth (Star: "Actually, my new show's terrible, a real turkey, but I'm hooked on pills, I've got three alimony cheques to write each month, and I owed the network boss a favour because I accidentally impregnated his daughter"). It's an event at which every new sitcom is described as brilliant, as *hee*-larious, as having prompted such violent and prolonged bursts of cacophonous laughilarity during test showings that several audience members are still scouring the screening room in a frantic attempt to find their lungs. That's the unspoken deal: the networks tell the critics how awesomely great their new shows are going to be and, in return, the critics agree not to call them a bunch of lying dirtbags. Plus they dispense free alcohol.

Ah, yes, the alcohol. An integral component of the Press Tour is the alcohol, which is made available during each network's obligatory "all-star" party. Celebrities such as Drew Carey can be expected to show up at such affairs and chat with TV writers, at least until Rebecca Romijn-Stamos walks by, at which point, true story, Carey will depart mid-sentence to inspect the actress/lingerie model from a more intimate vantage. It is only the soothing presence of much complimentary alcohol in the bloodstream that enables the television critic to shrug off this sort of callous behaviour.

The "all-star" parties can be awkward, forced affairs, and are typically characterized by the sight of publicists wandering around and trying to read the ID card that hangs around the neck of each accredited guest, a tactic used to determine whether the critic works for a publication of sufficient influence that his existence as a human being should be acknowledged. To their credit, the publicists never try to pretend they're doing anything other than that. Once identified, the critics and reporters who toil for *USA Today* or *Entertainment Weekly* or other major media players are subsequently accosted with a stable of provocatively clad ingenues and tight-shirted, aspiring mandroids, each desperate to be declared Hot, or It, or, at the very least, on the verge of Hotness or Itness. Everyone else spends their time drinking mojitos, chatting amiably with famous people, and covertly tailing Lara Flynn Boyle on the off chance that they might witness the consumption of her biweekly stalk of celery.

What's most intriguing about the "all-star" party is that it is one of the rare forums in which you can observe the behaviour of so many people who are utterly convinced that they are poised to become hugely rich and globally famous. Being congenitally cynical, critics understand that in spite of the prevailing mood of sunny optimism during the Press Tour, despite all the upbeat adjectives network executives have deployed to describe their new shows and all those involved in them as next big things, more likely than not a series will not make it to a second season. Actors and creative types know the odds better than anyone, but the thrill of finding oneself on the verge of wealth and celebrity tends to diminish one's fondness for mundane interjections of reality.

The ABC party in the summer of 2002 was memorable for a rather enthusiastic late-night dance session involving the (mostly) inebriated cast and production team from *That Was Then*, a time-travel drama that was to air on Friday nights. Cast members spoke about having landed their big break. They talked about which expensive imported automobile they intended to purchase. By the end of the night, one actor was even experimenting with expressions of disdain for the intrusive and boneheaded queries of the press corps. "I've had just about enough of the 'So how excited are you?' question," he lamented to a castmate. Not a problem: *That Was Then* did indeed air on Friday nights – two of them, to be precise. Two episodes were broadcast and then it was cancelled. The young cast members were abruptly returned to the land of auditions and odd jobs, that familiar place where the pertinent question is not "Mercedes or BMW?" but rather "Would you like fries with that?" No word on whether that actor has yet grown weary of the 'So can you work the all-night drive-thru shift?' question.

That same ABC party also presented the rare opportunity for mere mortals to witness famous people interacting with other famous people. The network was aggressively promoting its new late-night talk show, which would debut six months later, with Jimmy Kimmel as host. Kimmel came to fame, and more often to infamy, as co-host of *The Man Show*, a Comedy Central confection that swiftly became renowned for its set, which featured bikini-clad women bouncing on trampolines, and for its scatological sensibilities. On one episode, Kimmel and his colleague, Adam Carolla, placed money in a public toilet filled with fecal matter, and set up a hidden camera to forever answer the question of how far some men will go for twenty bucks. Naturally, this prompted ABC executives to perceive Kimmel as the obvious guy to follow Ted Koppel. "It's a great opportunity," Kimmel said of his talk show, "but I dread what will happen if it goes badly. It's an unforgiving business – you fail and you're done forever." He stared at the floor. "I mean, Pat Sajak went right back to *Wheel of Fortune*, and he's *never* leaving."

Which brings us to a multiple-choice question from the final exam in Public Relations 101: You are a PR agent in the employ of ABC, a major American broadcast network that has convened a huge party so that its stars and producers might mingle with drunken television writers. You are assigned to accompany Trista Rehn, who gained international fame as one of the desperate women on the reality series *The Bachelor*, and who was, in early 2003, the floozer instead of the floozie on *The Bachelorette*. While at the party, you spot Jimmy Kimmel, a man whose CV has yet to be adorned with the Man of the Year award from the National Organization for Women.

Do you (a) run for your professional life; (b) fatally wound Kimmel with a chicken skewer and then run for your professional life; (c) grab Trista by the arm, guide her right over to Kimmel and say, "Hi, Jimmy, this is Trista!"

The correct answer, of course, is (b). Or (a). Or basically anything other than (c), a scenario which, were it novelized and shipped to bookstores, would surely bear the title *This Can Only End Badly*. And it did. End badly, that is. As a dozen or more curious people gathered round – as even ABC chairman Lloyd Braun leaned in, saying, "This I gotta hear!" – Jimmy Kimmel met Trista Rehn.

JIMMY: I think that what you really need to do [during *The Bachelorette*] is immediately have sex with at least one of the men. That'll get me to watch.

TRISTA: *Frozen smile.*

JIMMY: You're not a lesbian, are you?

TRISTA: *Frozen smile. Eyes darting in search of someone, anyone, who will come to her rescue. Help! Damsel here! In distress!*

JIMMY: Good luck to you. I hope it doesn't go horribly wrong and you're boxing someone in a year.

TRISTA: *A wave of relief crosses her face as she is spirited away by that same publicist, although not before revealing that she's already been approached by, and has rejected, the fine people from* Celebrity Boxing.

A few days later, Fox held its gathering at Skybar, a preposterously trendy outdoor nightspot created by Rande Gerber, husband to Cindy Crawford. It was an opportunity for television critics to rub elbows – and, as the Sunset Boulevard joint grew increasingly crowded, shoulders, thighs, and, on rare and pleasant occasion, even bosoms – with the network's roster of prime-time thespians. The place was packed, and there is little doubt that the following morning and for days after that a large contingent of specially trained operatives was retained to remove from the establishment that lingering, low-rent TV-critic vibe.

The rooftop Skybar offers a spectacular view of Los Angeles and the Hollywood Hills and, on this night at least, the cleavage of Jeri Ryan of *Boston Public*, who in choosing her outfit for the evening demonstrated a keen affection for the hot new fashion label, Check Out My Awesome Rack! Over by the windows, a trio of women applied complimentary henna body decoration to game passersby. There were small futons all over the place, and throw pillows, although none was positioned close enough to the bar to break one's fall upon being informed that, on a regular night of business, a martini costs eighteen dollars (U.S.).

Up a flight of stairs was the pool – or rather, as the proprietors insisted on calling it, the Water Salon. On this night, in waist-deep water, stood two men and two women, all of them beautiful, each adorned in a red swimsuit and tank top, each assigned the task of diving to the pool floor to fetch for each patron a small piece of orange plastic, on which was inscribed a fortune. "Go for it," read one; another proclaimed, "The love of your life is sitting to the left of you." (Clearly, the author of these fortunes never imagined a scenario in which the person to the left would be a chubby, bearded TV critic from Portland.) Amusing enough, but it would have been far more helpful had each conveyed the critical message, "Even though the booze is free for the purposes of this function, the attractive cocktail waitresses will glare a hole through your face if you do not tip them generously, you cheap bastards."

The conversation was typical for this sort of affair. To get a sense of it, I started at one end of Skybar and walked to the other, jotting down every fragment of chatter that I heard. Here is what I ended up with: "spiritual-level growth," "he's a total dick," "that kind of money is an insult," "it's an apple martini," "right on, brother" (uttered by a thirtysomething white man), "the auditioning process is brutal" (uttered by Ron Glass, best known for his stint as Detective Harris on *Barney Miller*; he had won a role in Joss Whedon's short-lived sci-fi show, *Firefly*), "I'd rather be at the *Austin Powers* premiere," and "that's not standard on the Lexus. No, it doesn't come standard!" Along the way, I saw two different people make the same gesture (hands clasped together and then rocked gently, backward and forward), and later went back to investigate. It is, I was informed, the new way of indicating "I'm not worthy," and it's become a fashionable way to depart an industry conversation. I gave it a try. *Fabulous!*

The odd thing about being in Hollywood, in a bar chock full o' television executives and television stars and television publicists, is that it is one of the more difficult places in which to have a decent conversation about television. Well, that's not entirely true: you can find people who will yammer at great length about the industry, about who's hot, whose show is getting picked up, who bombed an audition, who got a little extra grabby during a sex scene. Everyone knows and delights in discussing the buzz. But there are awkward silences aplenty when it comes to TV itself, the medium, the thing we in the real world stare at hour after hour each night. It is an accepted industry custom, you see, that no one who works in television actually watches television.

It is a recurring theme in the Q&A sessions that dominate the Press Tour: I don't get the chance to watch much TV, I haven't seen that show, I'm not familiar with that series, I'm too busy to have watched it, but I hear good things about it. As Andy Richter, who starred briefly in Fox's *Andy Richter Controls the Universe*, offered by way of explanation: "My step-father was a plumber, and when he came home, the last thing he ever wanted to do was fix the sink. Personally, as an actor, I'd rather read a car magazine or something than watch TV."

Back at Skybar, the fabulousness began to expire around eleven o'clock. The water nymphs towelled off, the Fox executives left the bar, and all of a sudden the acquiring of an alcoholic beverage required cash – or, if you happened to be buying a round, a second mortgage. As word got around, the place cleared out quicker than Muskoka on Labour Day. Like many in the crowd, I took a fleeting look back at the futons, the pillows, the eighteen-dollar martinis, the cocktail wait-resses serving the eighteen-dollar martinis, and the general all-round abundant fabulousness of it all. And then I headed back to the hotel to watch TV. Somebody in this town has to do it.

It certainly wouldn't be the people who were up on stage at the Press Tour. Most of them were far too occupied with taking themselves far too seriously, a full-time job in Hollywood. Consider the summer of 2002, when the big hit was *American*

Idol: The Search for a Superstar, a show that blended the nostalgic appeal of a 1950s talent search with the contemporary fervour for acerbic criticism and young, attractive women whose clothes never manage to conceal their navels. Keen to promote the final episodes before America selected its Idol, Fox trotted out the show's producers, its trio of judges, and the eight remaining contestants. It would be, network officials gravely advised that morning, the final chance to speak with competitors before the conclusion of the series, which at that point was almost two months away.

Actually, the warnings had commenced sixteen hours earlier. "I have an important announcement," a Fox flack said the day before the *American Idol* contingent appeared. His solemn tone made Cronkite's pronouncement of JFK's passing seem jocular by comparison. "Tomorrow morning will be the last time that the final contestants will be available." Actually, he said it more like this: "The. Last. Time." Critics were left to insert imaginary bursts of ominous orchestral music.

One restless night later (Our last chance? Who could sleep?!), anxious and overcaffeinated, more than two hundred critics gathered to await the arrival of A.J. and RJ (EJay, alas, had been voted off by viewers a week earlier, thus diminishing J-related confusion) and the rest of the aspiring pop tarts. But first, another announcement. It is a custom that the people who come to plug their shows stick around afterwards for a bit, to mingle with reporters, answer a few more puffball queries, and otherwise perpetuate the fiction that they don't consider the people who write about their shows to be the entertainment industry's equivalent of chronic shingles. John Wells, one of the busiest and most successful producers in television, stayed and chatted that July. So did Ben Affleck, who came to promote the ill-fated series that he helped create (ABC's *Push, Nevada*). But the Fox flack, adopting the stoic inflection of a man doing voice-over work on a Depends commercial, informed critics that the eight *American Idol* finalists would be escorted from the stage at the end of the Q&A. Bummer! Perhaps the classroom called: More urgent lessons in Earnest Gazing into a Far-off Nothingness, Dramatic Fistpumping, and Mildly Arousing Yet Ultimately Non-Threatening Booty Shakin'.

Of course, the truth is that *American Idol* discovered its superstar in its very first episode. He was Simon Cowell, the frank, villainous Brit who served as one of the show's judges, and without whom the series would have embarked on a voyage to the bottom of the Nielsens. Cowell's heartless dismissal of contestants ("You were awful," "That was dreadful," and so on; once asked by a singer to "help remake me," Cowell held up his pen and said, "It's not a magic wand") was the show's signature element and, more important still, a jarring counterpoint to the rampant giddiness of the performers. This is, after all, the recording industry we're talking about, a business not exactly renowned for its kitten-soft snugability. "The music business is illogical, it's sexist – that's just the way it is," Cowell told us. "And I'm the person who's there to remind everyone of that. I wouldn't be serving anyone's interest if I were dishonest."

Paula Abdul, a former pop tart herself and another of the judges, feuded with Cowell, though her purported dislike of him mostly came off as a pro-wrestling-style concoction. At one point during the session with critics, Abdul described herself as "the link of empathy" on the panel of judges, a declaration that prompted Cowell to roll his eyes with theatrical vigour. Later, when a reporter brought up the fact that Cowell described Abdul as interested not in the search for a superstar but only in the search for a husband, she replied, "All I know is that since the show started, seventy men have called me and only twenty-three men have called Simon." Zing!

There were questions for the contestants, too, and we were delighted to discover at the time that they all got along just great, everyone hung out together and helped one another, nobody hated or was jealous of anyone else, and the whole gang was pretty much dedicated to keepin' it real. Dawg. "We all pray together as a group," said A.J., or possibly RJ (there was definitely a J involved). "We lift each other up with Scripture."

And with that, they were gone. True to the network's word, the contestants were spirited from the stage with a sort of precision and gusto that seemed cribbed from the Secret Service handbook, chapter five, subsection 32: "How to React When President Confronted With Hail of Machine-Gun Fire." One American reporter tried to ask contestant Ryan Starr about her outfit, which consisted of a pair of jeans, a red studded belt, and what appeared to be a meticulously positioned fabric swatch, but the poor girl was hustled along like a dawdler in an abattoir's cattle chute. Cowell stuck around, however. The meat had departed, but we could still chat with the butcher.

Speaking of cut-ups: "Can I tell you a funny story?" Drew Carey asked a small group of television critics. By this late stage of the 2002 Press Tour, we were far more accustomed to pointless, tedious, and self-aggrandizing yarns involving "irresistible scripts" and "incredible casts," but we nevertheless acquiesced. So Carey began.

New York. Mid-May 2002. Carey and many other ABC stars are gathered for what's known as the upfronts, the annual week during which networks unveil their fall shows to advertisers. After the presentation, Carey climbs into a limousine with Jim Belushi, Carey's co-star Kathy Kinney, and at least a half-dozen other people. As the car pulls away, the talk turns to time slots. It has just been revealed that *The Drew Carey Show* is moving to Monday nights. "Who's taking your old slot on Wednesday?" Belushi asks. Carey replies, "*The Bachelor.*" And then Carey begins to rant about the successful reality series, which had recently aired to strong ratings.

"Can you believe this fucking guy?" he says to Belushi and to all who had packed into the limo. "Twenty-five women to choose from, all of them really smart and educated, and who does he pick for the last two? The two blondes with the biggest tits." Carey went on: "I mean, the one fucks him, so that's the one who wins. The one that doesn't come across, she gets swept by the wayside. She loses the whole game." At this point the fellow sitting next to Carey interrupts. "Actually, that's not exactly how it happened," the man says. There is a brief silence, and then Kinney – the actress who played Mimi on *The Drew Carey Show* – looks up at the man and exclaims, "That's him! That's the Bachelor!"

Says Carey, "He was sitting right next to me the whole time, and I swear to God, you know, I thought he was Jim Belushi's agent, because he looked like an agent to me. He had the slick hair and stuff. . . . I didn't see any of the [*Bachelor*] shows. But the whole time I was going off, I noticed everybody's faces are kind of like, 'What are you doing?' Because he was, like, right there."

What does this encounter tell us about Hollywood, about fame, about celebrity? Well, it confirms our worst fears, doesn't it? No matter how famous a person becomes, no matter how many millions of dollars he has earned, he may still be obliged to share a limo with Jim Belushi.

More than publicity or creativity or open bars – more than anything else, really – the Press Tour is about ego: indulging it, exercising it, and, not infrequently, crushing it, three pastimes in which most Hollywood personalities could conduct a master class. Take, for instance, John Walsh, host of *America's Most Wanted*, who during the summer of 2002 was promoting the forthcoming debut of his daily, hour-long syndicated series, *The John Walsh Show*. Walsh has long had a tight bond with law-enforcement officials, to the point that he was the only TV personality to visit Ground Zero in the immediate aftermath of September 11. How do I know this? How can I possibly know Walsh was the only one? I know this because

I am a Professional Journalist, trained to listen for even the most subtle of verbal clues and capable of blending "hint" and "supposition" to reliably produce "fact."

These cryptic comments are excerpted from Walsh's remarks to reporters during a breakfast session at the Press Tour:

8:10 "I was the only media person allowed down there."

8:11 "The FBI sent for me, and nobody was allowed to go down to Ground Zero, and I was down there."

8:12 "I was the only person given permission to go down there."

8:17 ". . . having been at Ground Zero and being the only guy allowed there. . . ."

8:18 "I went down to Ground Zero and was the only guy that was allowed there."

Based on my expertise in deciphering, I can also confirm that Walsh was the only reporter allowed at the site of the Oklahoma City bombing and the only reporter to ride with an elite squad of Florida county investigators.

8:21 "I had been at the Oklahoma bombing. I was the only guy allowed down there."

8:22 "I went to the Oklahoma bombing . . . and I was there alone."

8:25 "I was riding with the Broward [Fla.] Fugitive Squad, and they don't allow anybody to ride with them."

As breakfast with John Walsh suggests, the television business is much different from television, and typically far more entertaining. Certainly, few would possess the mindset, let alone the titanic ego, required to marshal a nation's two most horrific and lethal terrorist attacks into the service of establishing one's cred as a syndicated daytime talk-show host. Ego is a currency in Hollywood, an intangible form of legal tender that can seal a potential business transaction. But it's also a currency in which one can go from boom to bust in a single morning. Just ask Mike White.

The young executive producer's moment had arrived. He was on a stage in front of a couple hundred television writers, sitting alongside Dana Delany and other members of the cast for *Pasadena*, White's prime-time drama that would debut two months later, in the fall of 2001. Fox honchos had earlier pronounced themselves "quite excited" about the executive producer's first series, which chronicled the fictional lives of some of the wealthiest residents of the Los Angeles suburb. The session went well. White was charming and funny. Delany killed with her impression of the hands-off approach favoured by Diane Keaton, who directed the pilot episode ("My imitation of Diane is, 'OK, we're all rich! [*giddy squeal*] Action!'"). Afterwards, a smiling White was surrounded by curious reporters. If the title hadn't already been spoken for, it's likely White would have proclaimed himself King of the World. A short time later, in a nearby conference room, White – his countenance completely reassembled, like a Mr. Potato Head whose smile had been exchanged for a frown – was spotted in the company of a Fox executive. They were flipping through a script for an episode of *Pasadena*. With each turn of a page, the executive made a remark along the lines of "More tension! We need more tension!" or "Mystery! There's not enough mystery!" And on. And on. For the better part of half an hour, it went on: "Tension!" "Mystery!" "Make it more extreme!" The tone was scolding and impatient. One minute, Mike White was King of the World. The next, he's not even King of His Own Show. Two months later, Fox aired a few episodes of *Pasadena*. The ratings were awful, and the network pulled the drama, suggesting it might one day return. It didn't, of course. There was never any hope it would.

The following year, Dana Delany killed again – this time in promoting her role as one of the leads in the new medical drama *Presidio Med*. CBS was said to be "quite excited" about the show. Halfway through the season, the network pulled the drama, suggesting it might one day return.

COMING UP DURING
SWEEPS MONTH

Three times a year, the American television networks participate in something called Sweeps Month, a period during
which ratings are even more important than usual. Let me put
that in some sort of context for you. If a show receives poor
ratings during non-Sweeps months, it will swiftly be cancelled. A show that receives poor ratings during Sweeps
Month will swiftly be cancelled, and its cast and producers
will be mortally wounded with a lance. That's because a
network's performance during Sweeps tends to determine
how much it can charge for commercials. And how much a
network charges for commercials tends to determine whether
the head of that network is paid enough to bathe (a) in Evian
water, or (b) in Evian water with two high-priced call girls.

That's why you see so many celebrity guest stars on prime-
time series during Sweeps Month. That's why you see so many
momentous occasions and so many can't-miss developments
and so many physically fit gentlemen taking off their shirts for
dubious reasons. And that's why it wouldn't be surprising to
see any of this:

Friends: Having exhausted nearly every possible angle for
intra-group romance, having depleted the stock of timeless

sitcom plot devices such as the Wedding and the Baby, the writing staff of this veteran show employs the only genuine ratings-grabbing gimmick left at its disposal: Orgy.

America's Most Wanted: In what was intended to be an amusing prank by *AMW* staffers, the physical description of a suspected mass murderer is amended to match that of host John Walsh, who is subsequently lynched live on national television. Fox immediately releases a statement decrying the senselessness of the tragedy – and announcing that footage of the brutal slaying will be aired again next Wednesday as the centrepiece of a two-hour prime-time television event.

The West Wing: In an effort to attract more viewers among those in the younger demographic, the show's writers pen a Very Special Episode that chronicles President Bartlet's controversial decision to sign an executive order mandating the reunification of Britney and Justin.

Survivor: In the latest and most highly anticipated instalment of the reality series, sixteen Americans are abandoned on some of the most vast, inhospitable terrain on the face of the earth: Marlon Brando's jowls.

60 Minutes: The venerable newsmagazine attempts to bolster ratings by employing an unprecedented season-ending gimmick of its own: just before Andy Rooney rifles through the crap in his desk for the eighty-fourth time, Mike Wallace fills one of the drawers with scorpions.

The District: There are no gimmicks at all planned for this series, a fact that will come as no surprise to veteran observers of the television industry. After all, it is integral to the national security of the United States that the show continue to attract, as it has since its debut, precisely zero viewers. That way, the FBI can continue to use the time slot to broadcast crucial, eyes-only video messages to its undercover field agents.

Frasier: Keen to rekindle the sparks of romantic tension that drove the show before Niles and Daphne finally got together, the groundwork for a month of Very Extra-Special Episodes is laid when a suddenly smitten Frasier swallows hard and stares into the deep, welcoming eyes of Eddie.

Cops: In an effort to draw viewers to this aging series, the producers may have no option but to move forward their annual episode on which a white guy gets busted.

Law & Order: Loyal viewers won't want to miss this milestone: during the obligatory conversation between the District Attorney and his underlings, balloons will descend and celebratory sirens blare as the D.A. gruffly utters the phrase "You need more evidence!" for the thousandth time.

Boomtown: In a novel attempt to enlarge its audience, the cop drama will, as usual, chronicle a crime and the ensuing investigation from the perspectives of the police, the criminals, the politicians, and the media. Except this time, they all happen to see the same thing: a scantily clad Tyra Banks.

Meet the Press: In order to enliven the typically staid Sunday talk show, producers coax a Democratic presidential candidate to swipe Tim Russert's pen during a commercial break. Moments later, during the show, a perplexed Russert asks, "Hey, has anyone seen my pen?" At which point the candidate replies, "Yes, I have it," and hands it over. And then everyone chuckles thoughtfully.

Monday Night Football: In a gambit designed to attract more female viewers to the telecast, sometime during the third quarter of tonight's game Gilbert Brown, a 350-pound lineman for the Green Bay Packers, will be caught up in a steamy love triangle involving John Madden and a rack of lamb.

Fear Factor: The popular reality series descends on Washington, D.C., for a special two-hour episode featuring six members of Congress. Participants will be challenged to perform such terrifying and unthinkable feats as "actually talking with a voter" and "shutting the hell up for four minutes."

CELEBRITY GENITALS

Opening credits: A generic orchestral ditty plays over a series of elegant soft-focus black-and-white photographs: Click! Lorenzo Lamas in a thong. Click! Mr. T gingerly shaving his pubic area into a mohawk! Click! Bea Arthur sprawled naked on a bed, her feet resting in stirrups! Title card: Celebrity Genitals. Created and executive produced by Dick Clark.

ROBIN LEACH (*hoisting a glass of champagne*): Cheers, and welcome to Beverly Hills, playground of the rich and famous! Tonight on *Celebrity Genitals*, we pay another lengthy visit to the popular, welcoming confines of Winona Ryder's vagina. And we dispatch our essayist, William F. Buckley, Jr., to document the meticulous vulva of Ms. Jennifer Tilly. But first: He's a member of one of America's great acting families. He's shared the screen with such world-renowned beauties as Sharon Stone and Cindy Crawford. He's got a palatial home in Beverly Hills, a remarkable collection of exotic cars, and, as we'll discover tonight, one spectacular penis and two awe-inspiring testicles. Join me as we embark on an exclusive tour of the genitalia of Billy Baldwin!
Robin and Billy sit in the den of Billy's magnificent Beverly Hills estate. A log fire crackles in the background. Robin wears a

double-breasted blue blazer and grey flannels. Billy wears a gym
sock over the dangly elements of his crotch.

ROBIN: Thanks for agreeing to show our viewers around your privates, William. It's such a privilege for me and for them.

BILLY (*smiling proudly*): It's my pleasure, Robin. I'm glad you finally returned my calls.

ROBIN: Well, we were up at Schwarzenegger's mansion for a whole week, and you can imagine how that was. [*Adopts crude Austrian accent*] Do you haf eenuf pictoors ov my spektahcu-loor gonahds, Rawbin?! De're flawlessly symmetricul, Rawbin! Maria, fetch de bahby oil to mahke dem shine!

BILLY (*absently caressing himself*): Well, I'm not sure how mine will compare to the Terminator's. I mean, they're just my boys, you know. They're nothing special.

The Steadicam operator draws near as a production assistant slowly, teasingly, removes the sock.

ROBIN (*voice-over*): Billy's just being modest – non-famous men would kill for a set of balls like that!

Baldwin's genitalia are lovingly photographed from a variety of angles. Music: "Can't Touch This!"

ROBIN (*V/O*): The shaft: long and elegant, reminiscent both of the architecture of ancient Greece and the throbbing manhood of a young Dick Van Patten. The head: in perfect proportion to the shaft; robust and regal, with a happy, buffed exterior that practically exclaims *Sophistication!* If they gave out Oscars for Best Pantload, Billy Baldwin's mantel would be chock-ablock with golden statuettes!

A Teamster grasps Billy's legs and hoists them above the actor's head, allowing the Steadicam operator to continue his rigorous documentation. Billy wiles away the time by reading a John Grisham novel.

ROBIN (*V/O*): Yes, it's a world-class penis. But Billy's pride and joy is the fleshy, wrinkled sac in which his testicles spend their day, luxuriously enshrined within a silky-smooth epidermis that would be the envy of the Pharaohs themselves!

BILLY (*looking up from book*): Harrison Ford has a scrotum just like it.

ROBIN (*V/O*): Befitting its superstar status, Billy's genitalia divide their time among a number of exotic and opulent domiciles, including these red silk boxers, these striking black briefs – fashioned from 750-count Egyptian cotton, no less – and this leopard-skin thong, which was given to him as a gift by the film director Martin Scorsese.

BILLY: But these – *these* are my favourites.

Billy uses a key to open a small, elegant wooden chest, from which he removes a pair of white, monogrammed Y-fronts. He winks seductively at the camera.

ROBIN (*V/O*): Ah, the legendary Paraiso Supremo De Los Testiculos! Each pair of these peerless undergarments is hand-stitched by El Salvadoran textile artisans, and comes standard with a Genital Serenity Compartment designed by I.M. Pei. To ensure the utmost in comfort, each compartment is crafted from the pelts of two Russian minks! Talk about living a life of luxury!

BILLY (*slightly cross*): Listen, don't get me wrong, I love the GSC. My penis loves the GSC. My balls love the GSC. But I told Pei: I'm of a certain . . . *magnitude*. I'm going to need three minks minimum, buddy! Maybe throw in a hamster pelt, too. But the guy's such a control freak, he wouldn't alter the sketches. He kept shouting at me, "Big enough for Stallone, big enough for you!" You know . . . whatever, dude.

ROBIN (*V/O*): Blessed by the gods of venereal allotment? Of course! But Billy does not take his gift for granted. He rigorously adheres to a strict protective regimen, allotting time in the morning and night to submerge his manliness in a thick, revitalizing solution of jojoba oil and cow-udder balm.

BILLY: Man, when I was young, I can remember letting my pubic hair, you know, just do whatever it wanted. Wild and free, kimosabe. Wild and free. I mean, I'd even let it air dry . . . which just completely blows my mind now.

ROBIN: The shimmering, velvety curls of youth are wasted on the young.

BILLY: Exactly, dude. Exactly.

ROBIN (*V/O*): The lush contours of Billy's genital area are now tended to daily by Fazrul Kumar, an elderly Indian stylist who schooled under the famous pubic innovator Sir Waldo Frankenshire, inventor of Sir Waldo's Testicle Floss – which at the time was the cutting edge in the genital maintenance of the male celebrity.

BILLY: Fazrul is the best. *The* best. I swear, he treats my testes as if they were his own. He used to style Brando's butt-cheek hair [*pause*], you know, until the accident.

Tinkly piano music is played over soft-focus shots of Fazrul gazing solemnly at his flattened, deformed left hand.

ROBIN (*V/O*): Tragically, Fazrul Kumar lost the use of his hand – and a blow dryer, which curiously was never recovered – when Marlon Brando abruptly sat down during the protracted grooming process on the set of *Apocalypse Now*. But that didn't stop Fazrul! He went from misfortune to fortune, parlaying his notoriety – and the fact that the state government pays 90 per cent of his salary as part of a hire-the-handicapped initiative – into a career as one of Hollywood's most sought-after genital stylists.

Fazrul takes a seat next to Billy.

FAZRUL (*nervous*): Mr. Billy has a nice willy!

BILLY: At first, I can remember thinking to myself, 'I'm devoting forty-five minutes each day to the grooming of my pubic hair. Isn't that a bit excessive?' And then I saw the dreadlocks!

FAZRUL (*nervous*): Nice willy! Mr. Billy! Billy willy!

Fazrul takes out a hair pick and begins to fluff Billy's pubic area.

BILLY (*gazing down approvingly*): The man's a magician.

FAZRUL: Willy Billy!

Shatner!

The Anna Nicole Smith Show season finale: talk about your cliffhangers! Will she or won't she? And how the heck can we be expected to wait five whole months to find out whether she says yes to her latest suitor, Wallace, the 104-year-old steel tycoon? More to the point, how can Wallace be expected to wait? His pelvis, which shattered with a sickening *thrack!* as he attempted to drop to one knee, could certainly benefit from some wifely TLC. He shrieked so loudly that Anna could barely concentrate as she admired the proffered diamond ring through her Bausch & Lomb 10x grading loupe.

After a couple of tedious episodes that tested the patience of even the most devoted of fans (even I confess to zoning out when Anna detailed her private, intimate feelings about the various luncheon meats – I mean, who cares that pimento has "a transcendent subtext"?), the finale had it all: Anna's abrupt breakup with Heinrich, the 98-year-old shipping magnate (a prenup? Heinrich, you cad!), and her sudden fairy-tale marriage to a 107-year-old Malaysian textiles baron, whose name we didn't catch. Thanks to E!, we were there for the ceremony, as well as the ritzy reception, the couple's honeymoon night, and, the following morning, the baron's elegant funeral. And the producers of *ER* wonder why they keep getting clobbered in the ratings.

Of course, given the number of *Osbournes* copycats that were rushed into production, not every celebrity-based reality series could become such a runaway success. In fact, the swiftly evolving *TV Guide* prime-time grid is testament to the wounded egos of the scarcely famous and probably no longer rich.

Consider E! Channel's *The Piscopos*. In its promos, *The Piscopos* promised frequent appearances by a corps of A-list showbiz pals, but only the most naive of viewers was fooled by the former *Saturday Night Live* star's crude crayon-drawn renderings of Tom Hanks, Julia Roberts, and That Bastard Eddie Murphy Who Never Calls Any More, Not Even Now That He's a Has-Been Too! Meantime, over on *The Eddie Murphy Show*, far too much of each episode was devoted to Murphy's urgent yet profoundly boring efforts to renew a restraining order against Piscopo. Both shows were cancelled after three episodes, although technically Piscopo scored more network air time this season, thanks to his featured appearances on *America's Most Wanted* and, the following week, on *Cops*.

VH1's *The David Crosby Show* initially won over the critics with its brash rejection of the traditional editing techniques of celebrity reality series. Instead, its producers touted the program as the medium's first real-time unscripted show, a gimmick which in itself cannot be said to be the reason for the show's dwindling audience and its subsequent cancellation.

After all, no one could have predicted we'd be four episodes in before Crosby got up from the dinner table. Alas, even then it was only to fetch a snack. And let's face it, it was luckless in the extreme that Crosby's five-show nap coincided with Sweeps Month.

Shatner! was the Sci-Fi Channel's entry into the genre, but in retrospect the producers should never have agreed to hand creative control to the former *Star Trek* captain, who promptly abandoned the program's "video scrapbook" concept and instead used the weekly hour of cable air time to broadcast his "geographical coordinates" repeatedly for the benefit of "any young and lovely thing who might want to beam herself over." Still, for enthusiasts of the *Star Trek* franchise, the program delivered the occasional nugget of intriguing trivia. During a rare moment of introspection, for instance, Shatner revealed that it was he – not show creator Gene Roddenberry – who suggested that, upon encountering each new alien species, Captain Kirk should act neither out of fear nor aggression, but instead out of a "healthy scientific curiosity" that would lead him to ascertain the precise location of its sex organs.

Not surprisingly, *Shatner!* routinely finished last in its time slot, behind even *The Guy Who Played Herb on WKRP*, a reality series that was doomed from the moment its few viewers realized that the show's creators had mistakenly spent three months filming the life of the Guy Who Played Les on *WKRP*.

The Guttenbergs also suffered from anemic ratings, and justifiably so. Steve Guttenberg's bitterness over his eroded celebrity was manifested in his frequent insistence on imbuing even his most ghastly cinematic vehicles with implausible thematic depth. "The ketchup-squirting scene in *Police Academy 4* wasn't just some juvenile hijinks, it was a comment on the self-defeating ideological apparatus of the post-industrial state," he told the camera, thoughtfully fingering his soul patch. "The French get it, man."

The highlight of the finale was footage from Guttenberg's ill-fated appearance on Fox's *Celebrity Boxing 7*, which concluded with Guttenberg being knocked unconscious by his large-breasted co-star from the *Police Academy* movies. The embarrassment was only heightened by the fact that the diminutive Guttenberg was not actually on the boxing card, but had merely showed up to watch the fights when he spotted his former colleague and rushed to embrace her, striking her chest with sufficient velocity to be propelled three rows back. He came to just in time to watch the final, barbarous blows of Wilford Brimley's savage beating at the hands of Bea Arthur.

Meanwhile, the season finale of the show that started it all, *The Osbournes*, proved that the series has tragically misplaced the eccentric magic that made it such a compelling spectacle in the first place. Viewers who posted messages on the Web in an *Osbournes* chat room suggested several potential explanations for the show's malaise: Ozzy's increased drug use; Ozzy's increased incoherence; the inexplicable addition to the family of a bespectacled young cousin named Oliver. It probably didn't help that nine of this season's thirteen episodes consisted in their entirety of negotiations regarding another potential season of *The Osbournes*.

THE REALITY OF TELEVISION: REALITY TELEVISION

Join me, won't you, on a brief yet edifying tour of the brain of a top network television executive.

Obligatory legal disclaimer: Frightening scenes within. May contain nuts. You must be this tall to ride this chapter.

Employ your machete to hack through the thick hair weave. Pierce the skin. Penetrate the bony casing. Snorkel the surprisingly large gap between skull and grey matter. Endeavour to avoid disturbing the larger sections of the brain, the ones labelled "Inventive Ways to Abuse Fearful Underlings" and "Hot Babes Who Need Work." Instead, head for that smaller, throbbing chunk over there, the part that used to house a sense of humour until, after years of sitting dormant, it was retrofitted to warehouse Things That Totally Bum Me Out.

I should establish at this juncture that it is not easy to bum out a top network executive. To the contrary: top network executives are wealthy and powerful, two adjectives that work like advanced supertoxins to break down and expertly destroy any intruding sentiments of bummed-outtedness. Granted, top network TV executives are not quite as wealthy and not quite as powerful as top film-industry executives (power, in this case, being defined as the ability to rewrite a script to include a scene where Charlize Theron removes her clothes), but they are plenty powerful nevertheless. Top network executives employ college graduates whose sole responsibility is to fetch bottles of imported water for top network executives. *That's* how powerful they are.

Yet, as you can see, the portion of the brain devoted to Things That Totally Bum Me Out has, in this specimen, developed an unsightly bulge, a reflection of the fact that it is currently exceeding its recommended capacity. If this particular top network executive is totally bummed out by even one more thing, his brain is going to need to find more space to accommodate the bummed-out process. I'm no expert, but I'd guess it would probably annex the neighbouring section, the one labelled "Gary Coleman's Home Phone Number." I don't think he'll be needing that any time soon.

What would totally bum out so wealthy and powerful a person as a top network executive? Well, there's the proliferation of rival TV channels, for one. And there's the popularity of the Internet. The reluctance of young people to embrace traditional network programming, the fact that digital recording devices such as TiVo may one day threaten to render traditional commercials obsolete, the soaring costs associated with the production of prime-time dramas and sitcoms, and the harrowing death of Maverick's pal Goose in *Top Gun*, which, to be fair, did happen an awful long time ago, but is just not the sort of tragedy you get over, man. This would not be nearly so grave a predicament were it not for the fact that, as a top network executive, fully two-thirds of all cranial functions are devoted to keeping a straight face when publicly stating that the network's upcoming lineup of "hot" new fall shows will ensure that it prevails and remains viable in the face of these many troubling trends. That figure rises to three-quarters after six of these "hot" new fall shows are summarily cancelled due to anemic ratings.

Happily, a fat naked man has come to the rescue of the top network executive. During the summer of 2000, North America could not avert its eyes from the doughy, digitally blurred buttocks of Richard Hatch, the dastardly schemer who, as part of the most remarkable television phenomenon since viewers collectively decided that Erik Estrada was no longer a sex symbol, spent thirty-nine days on a tropical island and waddled away with international fame, a million dollars, and, even months later, grains of sand falling out of various cracks and crannies. The finale of *Survivor*, which aired in August 2000, was watched by fifty million Americans. *Fifty million!* To put that in some sort of perspective, take the number of people who went to see the film *Pay It Forward* that summer, and then add fifty million. *That's* how many people watched the *Survivor* finale.

The popularity of the series did not go unnoticed in the executive offices of rival networks. Meetings were convened. Ratings data were analyzed. Virgins were sacrificed. (Okay, okay . . . that's not exactly true. Some of the girls had been to third base.) Finally, the implications of *Survivor*'s astonishing debut began to resonate. "So let me see if I've got this right," the network executive ventured. "These 'reality' programs you speak of, they can be produced quickly and easily. More importantly, they can be produced very cheaply. And people actually will want to watch." At which point he removed the noose from around his neck, fired several hundred employees (just to celebrate his rebirth as a potentate), and set to work at enlisting the sort of creative people who'd be capable of generating completely original ideas about how to rip off *Survivor* without being successfully sued. The reality of television was about to become reality television.

In the face of this onslaught, some of the television shows that had long indulged in reality – this reality being different from the reality of reality TV, by way of its actually having something to do with reality – began to give off an unmistakable waft of Eau de Nostalgie. Take *America's Funniest Home Videos*. Already a network staple for a decade, during which it was routinely described as the domain of the submoronic, the show suddenly seemed quaint and harmless when compared to the loutish behaviour and Machiavellian scheming of the new reality. By comparison, *AFHV* has always has been about abrupt, grievous trauma to human genitals. I recall watching one episode of *AFHV* that featured: a young girl nailing her father in the privates with an aluminum baseball bat; a young boy enthusiastically grabbing his dad's nuts with a pair of pliers; a member of a synchronized swimming trio attempting to surface, but inadvertently directing her head into the nether regions of one of her colleagues; a kid squaring himself while attempting to land an Evel Knievel–style jump on his bicycle; a young girl deciding that the appropriate way to awaken her napping father is to jump from a substantial height and land upon his groin.

It would be easy to describe *America's Funniest Home Videos* as mindless, lowbrow television programming. It would also be accurate and, quite possibly, a direct excerpt from thousands of critical reviews. But here is a dirty little secret that TV critics admit only late at night, high up inside the TV Critics Clubhouse, after the keg of Schlitz has been drained, after we've debated the relative hotness of the various *Law & Order* foxes, after we've sent two dozen large pizzas to the house of Aaron Spelling and a dozen red roses to the future gravesite of David Hasselhoff: *AFHV* is the genuine reality show, a series that aims no higher than to convey the absurdity of life. And it is one of the funniest and most reliably entertaining shows on television.

For this, we must assign credit to the citizens of the United States of America, who have over the years demonstrated that not only are they idiotic enough to repeatedly stick their hands into the cages of vicious zoo animals and climb up unsecured ladders and drive heavy machinery whilst profoundly intoxicated, they also are moronic enough to marry or hang out with the calibre of people who, in the aftermath of the often severe misfortune, keep the Handycam running and giggle girlishly instead of rushing to help.

It was shortly after the finale of *Survivor* that I was asked by the arts editor of my newspaper, the *National Post*, to start writing about television. I remember the day quite clearly –

not so much because of the assignment, but because my sofa overheard the phone conversation and made a clumsy, ultimately futile dash for the door. I didn't hold it against my leather-clad manifestation of Swedish ingenuity. We were going to be spending a lot more time together, and it would clearly be getting the bum end of this relationship.

I said yes. To my editor, that is. (To my IKEA sofa, I said, "Stay!") I said yes, I took the assignment, and then rushed to buy a satellite dish, an amenity that would afford me not only access to hundreds and hundreds of channels broadcasting from five different time zones, but also the opportunity to fulfil my lifelong dream of choosing not to watch *Oprah* five times a day instead of just once. Sweet, sweet contentment. But here's the thing about watching television for a living: it sounds immensely appealing in the abstract. Let me show you what I mean. Read this next sentence out loud, gruffly:

"[Your last name here], I've got a job for you: I want you to watch television for a living!"

See? You're thinking: Cool! See you later, spreadsheets or deep fryer or tedious manual labour! I'll be the person sitting in front of the tube, watching stuff and typing a bunch of stupid words about it. Yee-haw! I'm watching television for a living, Ma! But the thing about watching television for a living is that *you actually have to watch television*. Lots of television. And invariably, no matter how selective you are in determining what to watch, you are going to discover that a lot of what television has to offer is – oh, I think the French have a word that puts it best – *crappe*.

Shortly after starting on the beat, I received a courier package from the Television Critics Association, one of two organizations to which most critics belong (the other, the American Association for the Restoration of Feeling to One's Ass). Inside, there was a welcome basket that contained a leather-bound holder for my *TV Guide*, a six-pack of Preparation H, a whole box of Suntan in a Bottle (Slogan: "Unsuspecting friends will think you actually went outside!"), and, it being 2001, a plentiful array of derogatory adjectives to employ when writing dismissively about reality television. *Big Brother*: Atrocious! *The Mole*: Odious! *Survivor*: Atrodious! Or is it odrocious? Whatever it was, my heart just wasn't in it. Sure, the brainy course of action would have been to opine that the glut of ersatz reality was debauching the medium and, with every elimination round or tribal council, devouring precious brain cells that might be put to better use solving the Middle East conundrum or, failing that, the more perplexing matter of how Caramilk gets the soft, creamy caramel inside the luscious milk chocolate (could it be . . . *magic*?) But I was reluctant to characterize this trend so swiftly as the end of intelligent life as we know it. Let me put it to you in the form of a question: Can a broadcasting industry truly be subjected to further debasement once it has been complicit in the launch of seven different series starring McLean Stevenson?

Despite the advent of VCRs and DVD players and data recorders, television remains almost exclusively a medium of impermanence: hundreds of channels relentlessly broadcasting original material, much of which will never be seen again – unless (a) it winds up in syndication, in which it will never be seen again by a large audience, or (b) it winds up sandwiched between *The Love Boat* and *Mod Squad* on the digital-channel TV Land, in which case it will never be seen again by an uninebriated audience. Tom Green movies get heavily promoted DVD releases with seven hours of bonus flatulence and simulated buggery; the finest episodes of *The West Wing* get repeated maybe once, and usually during the summer, when even the most dedicated telephile is out on the deck drinking a Heineken and marvelling at the tan lines left by his sandals.

The result is a popular culture wherein the prevailing belief is, at all times, that television has never been more derivative, embarrassing, and moronic than it is at this particular time. The popularity of *Charlie's Angels* signalled the end of modern civilization as we know it. The popularity of *The Dukes of Hazzard* signalled the end of modern civilization as we know it. The popularity of *Married . . . with Children* signalled not only the end of modern civilization as we know it, but also the notion that we'd all be punished in the afterlife for permitting the resurgence of Ted McGinley's career. We've gone to hell in a handbasket so many times now that we have got enough bonus miles to take that summer vacation to purgatory.

In its infancy, reality TV was routinely portrayed as a threat to the future of humanity, but the truth is that in its earliest forms it was a far more viable threat to the future of celebrity. Reality television established itself as a minor sort of populist uprising, the democratization of celebrity. It was as though the fame franchise had been extended to all adult Americans. Suddenly, you did not need to be attractive or hard-bodied or talented or, in some cases, in possession of your original complement of teeth in order to dominate the pop-culture conversation. In the space of thirteen weeks, Richard Hatch became the naked, gooey manifestation of the greatest fears of the famous and the infamous. Was America finally coming to its senses?

In a word: *Asfreakingif.* Instead, reality TV began to create what might best be called a class of celebrity temps – average folk who are called on to be showcased and exploited for a brief period, and then abruptly sent back from whence they came, never to be heard from again unless they get arrested for drunk driving or pass a bogus cheque or something. After the first *American Idol* competition, it was announced that the show's finalists would soon embark on a twenty-eight-city tour of the United States. I remember thinking: How are those kids going to play that many cities in just fifteen minutes? For the first couple of years, it was *de rigueur* for a reality-show participant to proclaim an interest in pursuing a show-business career. *Survivor* or *Big Brother* or any number of other reality programs were perceived by contestants as a first step, a calling card, an open audition in front of millions of television viewers. But these shows have ultimately proved to be none of that. They do not offer auditions for celebrity. Rather, they offer a new and fleeting brand of celebrity. Warhol's maxim may need to be adjusted: In the future, everyone will be famous for fifteen episodes.

Take, for instance, Charlie Maher, a man whose sole claim to temporary fame was having been spurned in front of more than twenty million people, the sort of rejection not seen since Al Gore was abruptly dumped by Florida. In March 2003, barely a month after the finale of the reality series *The Bachelorette*, Charlie and his temporary celebrity arrived in Ottawa for an appearance at the National Women's Show, an event that sounds like a vaguely empowering sort of thing but in fact is one of those shows that provides the depressing answer to the question: How long will someone wait in a lineup for a complimentary orange wedge?

I went to see what sort of reaction Charlie would get, and I learned an important lesson that day. I learned that if you broker peace in a war zone or win the Nobel Prize for chemistry or develop a revolutionary cure for a chronic disease, you will, for the most part, continue to wander through life in utter anonymity. If, however, you are dumped by a hot babe on international television in front of more than twenty million people during the final episode of a popular reality series, you will, upon sauntering onstage for a half-hour Q&A in the capital of Canada, be damn near swept away by a tornado of lustful shrieking from several hundred frenzied, hooting women, one of whom slept outside the doors overnight to ensure she'd get a primo seat.

It turned out to be an edifying thirty minutes. I learned that if you are an attractive celebrity temp who was dumped by a hot babe on international television, you can say things like, "There's a lot of asymmetric information in this process" or offer a brief dissertation on how a U.S.-led war on Iraq will result in several attractive financial opportunities in the American stock market, and women will – so long as you're a handsome, roguish sort with slicked-back hair and snug trousers – actually nod and pretend to give a crap. Also, if you say something like "I'm freezing to death up here [in Ottawa]," many women will spontaneously offer to warm you up, nudge nudge.

Above all, I learned that a celebrity temp who agrees to appear at a National Women's Show will be asked the following questions:

"Do you regret anything from being on *The Bachelorette* and can I please have a hug omigod?!" (*No and yes.*)

"Would you move a little closer?" (*Yes.*)

"Will you unbutton your shirt?" (*No.*)

"Can I have your clone?" (*Undecided.*)

"Can you sign an autograph for our time capsule?" (*Yes.*)

"Can my mom have a hug?" (*Yes.*)

"Why can't every man be like you?" (*Humble chuckling.*)

Every man can't be like Charlie Maher, but dammit, network executives are trying! They're trying to increase production of celebrity temps. They're trying to give the world more Charlies – Charlies at whom frenzied women from Ottawa can shriek lustfully before going home and flipping on their televisions to determine at whom they'll be shrieking lustfully a month hence.

As a television critic, I have been afforded the opportunity to (a) receive soothing back rubs from Jonathan Frakes (I had tension knots; he was "between Star Trek conventions"), and (b) chronicle reality's toddler years, from its spectacular birth (CBS's *Survivor*) to unsteady steps (*Chains of Love* being watched by seven unfortunate shut-ins whose remote batteries happened to expire while surfing past UPN) to firm footing (Fox's *Joe Millionaire* being watched by forty million people). What follows are fifteen vignettes from several of the reality programs that aired on American television in the months and years after the success of *Survivor*. It is entirely possible that future generations will gaze upon these words, cluck disapprovingly, and remark, "You sad buggers actually watched that crap?" Do not, however, discount the possibility that TV viewers of the future will read of *Big Brother* and *Chains of Love* and *Temptation Island* and declare enviously, "Wow, TV sure was cerebral back then!"

1. Temptation Island (Fox), February 7, 2001

During the spring of 2001, Fox aired *Temptation Island* – on which three committed and scantily attired couples descended on paradise and voluntarily split up and for almost two weeks subjected themselves to the ardent wooing of assorted glistening hard-bodies – up against NBC's *The West Wing*, which at the time was widely perceived to be the best drama on network television. The prevailing consensus was that few viewers would have difficulty deciding which show to watch. But were the two series really all that different? Here is a minute-by-minute examination of episodes that aired simultaneously. On *The West Wing*,

President Jed Bartlet was poised to deliver his State of the Union address; on *Temptation Island*, Mandy, Valerie, and Shannon were poised to turf from the island an arrogant massage therapist named Sean.

9:05 Jed Bartlet enters Congress to the words, "Mr. Speaker, the President of the United States!" Dano enters the running for Shannon's affection with the words, "She's a partier!"

9:11 The President concludes his speech and a poll is conducted to determine what Americans think of the address. The third round of dating concludes and a poll is conducted to determine what the ten single ladies, who were placed on the island as temptresses, think of the three hunky dudes.

9:13 After an untimely mishap, press secretary C.J. Cregg is obliged to appear on national television while wearing no pants. All the women who remain on *Temptation Island* continue to appear on national television while wearing no pants.

9:15 Abbey, the President's wife, appears agitated as she repeatedly views a segment of video from the State of the Union speech. Mandy, the aspiring singer, appears agitated as she recalls viewing the videotape of her boyfriend Billy performing an impromptu striptease while hammered out of his tree.

9:17 Leo, the chief of staff, is forced to make a quick decision after being told that five U.S. drug agents have been abducted in Colombia. He chooses to summon major government officials, sighing, "This was almost a good night." Andy is forced to make a quick decision after being told that he'll pick first for the fourth round of dating. He chooses Elizabeth, sighing, "She's hot as hell."

9:20 Amid a frenzy of nighttime activity in the raucous polling centre, Josh urgently inquires, "When do I get numbers?!" Amid a frenzy of nighttime activity on the raucous island beach, Mandy urgently inquires, "Is this an orgy?!"

9:23 Donna urges Josh to ask out enchanting polling expert Joey Lucas. Mandy and Valerie urge Shannon to ask out studly "polling expert" Tom.

9:29 Sam awkwardly attempts to display his affection for Ainsley by telling her, "You're a blonde Republican girl and no one likes you." Vanessa awkwardly attempts to display her affection for Billy by picking up a tropical butterfly and gently running it between her breasts.

9:36 Toby and the First Lady duke it out over changes in the wording of the speech regarding Medicare and social security, the issues that Abbey views to be of paramount importance. Andy and Kaya duke it out over the fact that Kaya was massaging the tonsils of Megan, the former Laker Girl who Andy views to be of paramount foxiness. "I look like a jackass," Andy says in an erudite analysis. "Megan looks like a whore."

9:45 President Bartlet shows the stress of trying to determine how to save the lives of the captured agents. Billy shows the stress of trying to determine how to select his Ultimate Dream Date. "This whole process is literally killing me!" he exclaims.

9:53 The First Lady tearfully laments that her husband has apparently decided to run for a second term. Megan tearfully laments that her Kaya has apparently decided to choose sexy Alison for his dream date.

9:59 A preview of the next episode portends plenty of tension, frayed tempers and the prospect of the United States going to war. A preview of the next episode portends plenty of tension, frayed tempers, and the prospect of an ice cube being rubbed on the neck of a scantily clad woman.

2. Chains of Love (UPN), April 18, 2001

The fetching woman on the television was shown reading a book and playing the piano. Her name is Vanessa, and she was described in an onscreen caption as an Outspoken Intellectual. It's true, Vanessa conceded, she intimidates guys because she is just "too cerebral." This sagacious genius, this daunting bastion of scholarly acumen, then slipped into a leg iron and chained herself to three other women as well as to Andy, a Hollywood stuntman with the IQ of braised pork.

Was this some sort of Mensa initiation prank? In fact, it was the reality series *Chains of Love*. The rules were as simple as the participants: save for bathroom breaks, Stuntman Andy and his harem of hard-bodied tramps (in some episodes, it was a gal affixed to four man-dolts) would remain linked for up to four days by a long metal chain and their unfathomable desire to demean themselves in public. Every so often, the Locksmith – a 350-pound black man in wrap-around shades and permanent scowl – would stride silently into the camera frame, a signal for Stuntman to cut loose one of his blonde-bots. "Vanessa, Amy, Kerstin, or Nicki," the show's host said after Stuntman encountered the Locksmith for the first time. "Each is unique in their own way." Kind of like Stuntman's six brain cells.

There was cash involved, of course, though not very much of it. Stuntman was given ten thousand dollars and was expected to dole out loot to each of the whor– er, contestants as he gave them the boot. When Stuntman narrowed it down to one gal, he had to decide if he was keen to pursue a relationship. If so, he was obliged to surrender half the remaining dough, with no guarantee that his romantic bond consisted of anything other than a nickel-plated restraining device. If not, he could dispense as much of the money as he deemed fit, a rule that seemed rather unfair to these ladies in that Stuntman didn't come across as the sort who, you know, grasped how to count all that, you know, high.

"I like to do all that kind of cliché-ish guy stuff," Stuntman Andy (Stuntmandy?) revealed to us at the program's outset. "I'm attracted to people that can really tell me what they want." It was a shame the gals couldn't hear this, or they'd have known the key to victory was to repeatedly bellow in Stuntman's ear, "Be smarter!" Later, as Andy was taken by minivan to the mansion where he would sleep with four women for what he acknowledged would *probably* be the only time in his life, he enjoyed snacks prepared by his future chainmates. "I gotta tell you," he said solemnly to the camera, "I'm not a huge cookie fan." Alas, he was about to be fastened to a quartet of them.

Having had our fill of ham, we were served a generous helping of cheese. The show's host, Madison Michele, somberly intoned in voice-over, "A distant bell summons the group into the Ritual Room, where the chaining ceremony will begin." Irons were fastened. Locks were engaged. Innuendo involving Stuntman's "tomatoes" was uttered. Apparently determined to offer a penetrating commentary on the philosophical ramifications of this brave social experiment, Stuntman considered the chains and expounded on their deeper meaning: "You know, it's not like I can walk away from [the four women] when I don't want to be with them." At home, it suddenly dawned on us: So *that's* why they never let stuntmen say anything in the movies.

Up to this point, *Chains of Love* had had me worried. Having fallen for *Survivor*, been smitten with *Temptation Island*, having even succumbed to the peculiar allure of *Boot Camp*'s shrill antics, I was really beginning to wonder if my standards (never too lofty to begin with, as my encyclopedic knowledge of *A-Team* episodes will attest) had deteriorated to the ignoble point that I might have been on the verge of becoming the president of a major American television network. And so it was with profound relief that I realized towards the end of this debut episode that *Chains of Love* was a loathsome morsel of exploitative eye candy and, far worse than that, unfailingly tedious.

Stuntman was the mighty potentate, the autocrat who breezily passed his unique brand of halfwit judgement on each woman's shortcomings in esteem and attitude. "I don't know you long enough," he told the brainy Vanessa, suggesting also that he don't study proper grammar long enough neither, "but I'm going to do the best I can to throw out what I feel you are about." When Vanessa defended herself, Stuntman raised his hands: "Wow," he said, "I'm definitely getting rubbed the wrong way here."

Stuntman's disparaging remarks and boorish behaviour – the guy could be denied entry to a foreign country as a contaminated meat product – were mitigated only by the fact that the women stood for it, gamely going down on his finger or assenting to some under-the-sheet fondling lest they lose out on a few hundred bucks. During the final night in bed, with just Stuntman and his best gal and a few dozen metal links writhing under the covers, the following whispered conversation actually took place.

STUNTMAN: We need to have fun in this house. We may never see each other again.
CHAINETTE: I'm getting tired.
STUNTMAN: Hey, be nice to me.

We weren't privy to what happened next, but Stuntman woke the next morning evincing no signs of having been hoofed in the gonads. That's not surprising, I guess: as pimp, it's the network's job to make sure the john has a good time.

3. Surprise Weddings 2 (Fox), May 10, 2001
Six women stood on a stage in Las Vegas, each dolled up in a wedding dress, each about to ambush her fella with an

ultimatum. It was a *60 Minutes* meets Reverend Moon kind of thing, and each proposal played out with suitable assembly-line predictability. The girl bawled, the guy walked in from a darkened hallway – unknowing, to the forced chuckles of a studio audience – and adopted an expression not seen since running on a mate's sword went out of fashion as a preferred means of suicide. He was then swiftly escorted to a private chamber, wherein he could furiously rub his brow and silently lament the absence of a side arm.

Stacey was the most wretched harpy of the bunch. At first, her relationship with Dave seemed the stuff of authentic romance: she barely knew her man, yet quit her job and moved two thousand miles so they could shack up. But she later let slip minor details, such as the fact that seven days after she arrived – a time in which she madly set up house, buying towels and such – Dave moved back in with his parents. Oh, and the small fact that he actually begged her not to come to live with him, but she did anyway. "We have such magic, such fireworks," Stacey told the Fox cameras. "That has to be the basis for something." Yes, Stacey, it's called the eight weekly performances of Siegfried and Roy.

In some jurisdictions, Stacey would be considered a stalker. On Fox, she was called "courageous." Addressing Dave, she said, "I told you the night we met that we're soulmates." That's smoochy enough on the face of it, I suppose, but the way she said the word "told" suggested not "lovingly informed" but rather "sternly decreed." *Run, Dave! Run!* Stacey's final plea to Dave, conveyed through a video monitor into his cell, "No matter what life smacks us in the head with, as long as you're standing next to me, getting smacked just as hard, we can accomplish anything." That sentiment seemed about right for *Surprise Weddings 2*: a marriage built on the solid foundation of blunt trauma to the brain.

Stacey got her man, alas, and her wish. She was married on TV in a forty-second ceremony officiated by a man known only as the Captain, who had Jimmy Swaggart's voice and Wink Martindale's hair. Only one of the six needy gals didn't get hitched. Instead, Michelle got a pledge that she would indeed get married, but in a fairy-tale setting in front of family and friends. The Fox producers treated it as though the guy had beaten her with a tire iron.

4. Big Brother 2 (CBS), July 7, 2001

I had just seen *A.I. – Artificial Intelligence* when I sat down to watch the debut of *Big Brother 2*, the highly unanticipated sequel to the original reality-show Valium. As initial glimpses were offered of the twelve cast members, I couldn't help but think that William Hurt – who played the brainiac robot designer in Steven Spielberg's flick – would soon be along to provide more formal introductions. Any halfwit could recognize these contestants, each imbued with a single defining character trait, were crude replicas of human beings.

"Meet Autumn, part of our NeedyChick5000 series," I figured Hurt would intone. "We've revamped this model's Whining Protocols and enhanced her Man-Glomming operating system. Our scientists now estimate she'll shamelessly throw herself at one of these male appliances inside of forty-seven seconds, which represents a marked improvement over our corporate rivals, who still see waiting times of more than a minute with WinonaRyder v.7.1."

Once Hurt detached Autumn's robo-fingers from his belt buckle, he would continue: "And here's Justin, our most advanced Man-Droid ever. This model is outfitted with our proprietary T-Shirt Avoidance Imperative, thus guaranteeing maximum exposure of its well-defined abdominal muscles, which were sculpted by a team of twenty-seven Korean artisans at our design facility outside Taegu. And I think we've finally worked out the kinks on the Third-Person Reference Sub-routine. To my mind, it's not much of a Man-Droid if it can't say . . ."

And Hurt would flip a switch on Justin's back, prompting the Man-Droid to proclaim, "Oh yeah, Justin likes the ladies!"

Regrettably, Hurt was a no-show – he was probably still embracing his agent for having landed him a role in a movie that some people would actually see – which left viewers to gaze in befuddlement upon the congregated automatons, resigned to ponder the intricate craftsmanship that went into fashioning such copious chest hair for Bunky the Gay-Bot, and into developing the Homophobic Vocabulary Database that's imbedded in the clutter of southern-fried circuitry known as Kent, a state-of-the-art prototype from the innovative engineers at Robo-Redneck Corp.

The rules had changed for the *Big Brother* sequel, but one guideline remained sacrosanct: you must either be hot or a total freak to get on the show, and preferably a total freak who is, like, hot. The show took place in a house on a CBS sound stage, where the Flirty Dozen – one of whom would go home with five hundred thousand dollars, the rest of whom would have to settle for the parting gift of cooties – resided without the company of television or books or music or, from all evidence, an introvert. A contestant was eliminated each week by a vote of all those who remained. Cameras and microphones were positioned throughout the residence, an impressive assemblage of gadgetry designed to deprive contestants of their privacy and enable viewers to listen in on the erudite discourse, such as Kent's scholarly treatise on gender differences and their profound societal ramifications: "These chicks ain't chicks, man, these are guys – and competitive guys. They'll cut your nuts off!"

Not likely. CBS was clearly determined that all its fellows retain their genitalia, ideally so they could think with them. CBS wanted sex from *Big Brother 2*. Sex. Sex. Ssss! Xxxx! They forked out for a *Cops*-style blurring machine and, doggone it, they wanted to fuzz out some excited weenies and the like. Indeed, in the days before the show's premiere, Arnold Shapiro, the show's new executive producer, was boasting that he'd recruited an extremely competitive and uninhibited group. He pretty much promised randy encounters. He explicitly promised this *Big Brother* would be far more provocative and cutthroat than its predecessor, which was described by critics as unfailingly tedious and, after intensive clinical research, by the U.S. Food and Drug

Administration as the first-ever sedative to be administered via cathode rays.

I'm not sure the sequel got Bob Dole's dog yapping friskily, either. The first romantic encounter involved the handsome Dr. Will and a fetching realtor named Shannon, who happily related to us what she looks for in a guy: "It's, you know, TAA," she said. "You have to have great Teeth, you have to have a nice Ass, and you have to have a great Attitude." Shannon and Will flirted and touched and eventually went to bed together and . . . slept, leaving us to conclude as we gazed at the static night-vision image that the nicely caboosed, good-tempered doctor had failed to floss before turning in.

5. Celebrity Boxing (Fox), March 13, 2002

A hearty "Pshaw!" to those of you who caught wind of Fox's *Celebrity Boxing* and immediately concluded that the very existence of the program would serve to further blight the fetid crudhole that is American popular culture. Sight unseen, this network special was denounced as repulsive and cultur-ally odious, an affront to intelligence and to decency, not to mention to the word "celebrity," which used to be reserved for movie stars and sports heroes but now apparently applies even to those whose sole claim to repute was to have con-fronted Bill Clinton's weenie. To grouch in this manner, to lament the trailer-park horror of it all, was like viewing the glass jaw as half-broken instead of still capable of processing most soft cheeses. It was to ignore the unique ability of *Celebrity Boxing* to do good, to inspire, to embolden.

Take, for instance, the effect of *Celebrity Boxing* upon crack whores. If I were a crack whore and I were waking up after having watched *Celebrity Boxing*, I'd probably be saying to myself, "Well, sure, I'm a crack whore and all. I sexually service unhygienic strangers in a desperate attempt to generate just enough income to meet the relentless cravings of my debilitating drug addiction. *But at least I wasn't on* Celebrity Boxing." Let's see Dr. Phil get that kind of esteem-boosting results!

Just in case you're aware of any crack whores who might have missed the big special (unfortunately, Fox aired it during the prime crack-whoring hours), here is a handy recap. Read it aloud to a crack whore you know and watch her self-regard soar!

The Undercard

Danny Bonaduce ("Danny" from *The Partridge Family*) vs. Barry Williams ("Greg" from *The Brady Bunch*)

Williams enters the ring like a Roman gladiator – which is to say, with the ashen countenance of a man who understands that, for the passing amusement of the gathered throngs, he is about to be mauled to death by a ferocious animal. At the age of forty-two, Bonaduce is fit and lithe, and his gloved hands move in a preparatory flurry that suggests he has, at the very least, seen a boxing match before. Williams is forty-seven. The elastic waistband of his boxing trunks has been soundly defeated in the evening's first bout: the fight to contain his doughy midsection. Bursting from his corner, Barry's abject prancing suggests he has put his own personal spin on

Muhammad Ali's famous strategy: he is floating like a very, very gay butterfly, or at least he is until eight seconds have elapsed, at which point he is (a) visibly winded and (b) knocked to his arse by a Bonaduce jabbette (to call it a jab would be overselling it). And so it goes: in slo-mo replays, Barry's droopy boobs quake hypnotically, with each of Bonaduce's hooks landing like a 7.6 on the corporeal Richter. Halfway through the second round, Williams is felled by a "punch" that wouldn't have made an impression on a bowl of mashed potatoes. His corner man throws in the towel. Bonaduce drops and embraces his beaten rival, a gesture that's described by the Fox announcer as "classy." Just to put that remark into context, Fox is the network that described *Who Wants to Marry a Multimillionaire* as "a fairy tale."

Todd Bridges ("Willis" from *Diff'rent Strokes*) vs. Rob Van Winkle ("Vanilla Ice" from a very brief and unfortunate period of music history)

Bridges is described by the Fox commentary team as "knowing the mechanics of fighting." (Translation: He's black and he's been to prison.) Vanilla Ice, on the other hand, could safely be described as "knowing the mechanics of fighting like a girl." As he flits about the ring, the rapper's legs kick up behind him, and the coming-over-the-top manner in which he throws a punch suggests more than a passing familiarity with the strategic intricacies of a slap fight. Bridges beats the crap out of Van Winkle, who takes his standing eight-counts with a facial expression of sufficient vacancy to suggest his mandatory protective headgear was a good decade late in being applied.

The Main Event

Paula Jones (famous for claiming to have been propositioned by pantless Bill Clinton) vs. Tonya Harding (famous for connection to comically inept perpetrators of Nancy Kerrigan kneecapping)

A late addition to the card (when Amy Fisher was obliged to withdraw), Jones joked that she feared only for her nose, which had been sculpted down at no small expense from its original supersize version. In the ring, alas, it becomes clear Jones is not joking: she is deathly afraid Harding might shatter her snot locker. At first, Jones (who arrived in full makeup) turns her head when she sees an incoming mitt. *Pow!* Right in the ear. Again. And again. By the second round, Jones is in perpetual flight, scampering, dodging, fleeing. At one desperate juncture, she actually grabs the referee *and uses him as a human shield.* A frustrated Harding lands blow after blow on the back of her rival's head. Ultimately, Jones chooses to stand in place, head turned away, arms at her side. The referee doesn't know what to do. Harding doesn't seem to know what to do, either, until her nature asserts itself and she clobbers the stationary Jones with a crushing right to the melon.

The ref calls the fight. Jones sighs with relief through her elegant, refined nostrils. Harding is exuberant as the *Celebrity Boxing* championship belt is fastened around her waist.

"This," exclaims the Fox announcer, "will go into the books as a win for Tonya Harding!"

And he's right: it will go down that way in the books. Books like *Inspiring Tales for Otherwise Luckless Crack Whores.*

6. The Bachelor (ABC), episode two, April 4, 2002

During the opening moments of *The Bachelor*, a thirty-one-year-old Harvard grad named Alex – "One of the most eligible bachelors in the country!" – was introduced to twenty-five women, each of whom had been procured by the network as a potential real-life spouse for their star hunk. In return, Alex pledged to try really hard to fall in love and, ultimately, assuming he could locate Miss Right within the leather-panted, cleavage-flaunting crush of Miss Desperates and Miss Needys and Ms. Potential-Stalkers, to gallantly propose marriage during the sixth and final episode.

This climactic moment would in all likelihood be followed by the sight of the happy couple scampering off to assemble their wedding registry, a list of everything they lack and urgently require for their life together, things like dignity, class, and maybe some clever disguises so they can occasionally venture out in public without having to endure such stage-whispered utterances as, "Hey, there's that lame bachelor guy who married that skanky strumpet!"

At the end of each episode, Alex was supplied with a bunch of red roses, obliged to stand before his harem, and instructed to present a flower to each of the women he had not yet done humiliating. Two episodes into the series, for instance, there were fifteen contestants and just eight roses, which meant that seven women were destined to leave the ceremony empty-handed – which in a way was convenient, because it would leave one hand free to sign the "Girls of *The Bachelor*" contract that was doubtless tossed at them by *Playboy* on the way out.

The bulk of an early episode was devoted to chronicling a series of "fantasy dates" that were crafted to provide *The Bachelor* with a whole new forum in which to evaluate the contestants and, in turn, to provide the contestants with a whole new forum in which to publicly humiliate themselves. Despite having boasted that his hobbies are "swimming, skiing, and romance," Alex seemed rather distressed as he sat in the back of a stretch limo, moments before his first date. This anxiety may have had something to do with the fact that he would be dating five girls at a time during the next three days. "I'm a little nervous about the etiquette of a six-person date," the Bachelor conceded. "This is new to me." This candid admission permitted viewers to glean one important fact about Alex: he is not from Utah.

Back at the Ladies Villa, an enormous California mansion in which the floozies were ensconced (funny, all we ever seemed to see of the grand place was the hot tub), the first group of five prepared to join Alex on a private jet to Las Vegas. There was within the villa a profound sense of disquiet – and, given the number of hair dryers on the go, an explanation for the state's electricity crisis.

Katie, a sales rep for a power-tools company, enthused that "Vegas is my dream date!" although she later conceded that, in her dream, there were not usually four predatory women tousling the hair and over-laughing at the weak jokes of her fella. Meantime, LaNease talked strategy: "I don't know if I'm going to do anything special to try to get him alone," she told us. "I'll just give him that look, let him know that I'm there." LaNease, an actress, did not indicate whether the look she was giving as she said this was the same look she'd be giving Alex. One hoped not, for it seemed improbable in the extreme that the Bachelor would be won over by a look that said, Gosh, I Hope My Mom Isn't Watching This.

(During the Vegas date, LaNease became the first contestant to neck with the Bachelor. "I don't want to be seen as a guy who's just out to kiss all the girls," Alex later said, during a brief intermission from kissing all the girls.)

Another of the dates took place at a luxury spa and, judging from the video footage, was conceived and designed with the exclusive purpose of capturing lingering shots of mud-caked bosoms. Many of these lingering shots were of the mud-caked bosom of Amanda, a twenty-three-year-old event planner from rural Kansas, of whom our Ivy League–educated Bachelor was heard to proclaim, "She has an absolutely rockin' body!" Alex later confided that, at first, he wasn't certain "she knew what to do with it" – her body, that is – but had subsequently come around to the viewpoint that she most certainly does. Know what to do with it, that is. Her body.

At the villa, meanwhile, Shannon – needy, needy Shannon – was gushing that Alex had made her feel special on their date. Very special, in fact. But since then she'd heard that a lot of her rivals had also been made to feel special. The discovery of others feeling special had subsequently made Shannon feel much less special. She eventually said this to Alex, who stared blankly and then replied, "You're special."

Each week the ladies were reminded that they were under no obligation to continue. Should Alex extend a rose, the host decreed, you're free to reject it and walk away. The women paid this about as much heed as one of those terms-of-use forms on a computer: swiftly clicking "Agree" and moving on to mentally downloading more china patterns and bridal-gown designs. The Bachelor stared into the camera and critiqued their bodies and their personalities and their behaviour; the women, in turn, devoted not a moment to critiquing the Bachelor. He was handsome, he had a good job, and he might even be straight. That, apparently, was enough.

Only one woman could be right for him, but the Bachelor was right for all women.

7. The Bachelor, episode four, April 18, 2002

"I want to know about your boobs," Alex told Amanda as they rode through New York atop a double-decker bus. "Tell me the whole story. Start at the beginning."

This romantic sweet nothing was dispensed during the first of a trio of "dream dates" for the Bachelor – one with each of the three remaining women in contention to become the object of his televised marriage proposal. Amanda, a woman who had already revealed her torrid desire to dress up in her Wonder Woman costume and be ravished by Alex, happily fielded the bosom-related query. One was always larger than the other, she explained, so she had a "breast aug." (For those of a curious mind, she opted to "supersize" rather than "downsize.")

Alex later confessed to the camera that he prefers "things to be natural all the time," which seemed to be a strike against Amanda – or at least it did until Amanda offered Alex a private tour of her reconditioned knockers in a "fantasy" suite at the W Hotel (arranged, of course, by ABC, esteemed broadcast network and pimp service – now *that's* corporate convergence!). One of the last images we glimpsed – from a black-and-white surveillance camera in the boudoir – was of Alex phoning in a room-service order for chocolate syrup, caramel, ice cream . . . and a plastic sheet. "Next time," Amanda said in a video message taped the morning after, "dessert is on you."

Alex's date with the conservative, reticent Shannon took place at a ski resort. It was cold, forbidding, frigid . . . and the weather was chilly, too. Shannon refused to discuss sex, was reluctant to reveal herself in a swimsuit, and declined even to neck with the Bachelor, suggesting that to do so would "cheapen" the intimacy of kissing. "I have some big concerns," Alex said later, emphasizing the word "big." Two words, pal: cold shower.

His final date was with Trista, a dancer for the Miami Heat, and it began in a helicopter over the ocean, where Alex managed to spot a couple of whales before puking inelegantly into a barf bag. This, alas, put something of a damper on the Bachelor's plans for further sexual conquest, although Trista's admission that she's "never had an orgasm during real intercourse" did seem to briefly inspire Alex to experience, well, *big* concerns.

To the surprise of no one in the viewing audience, Alex dumped Shannon on Invitation Night, leaving the Bachelor one episode in which to make three important decisions: whether to propose, to whom to propose, and to which country he and his new wife should immediately emigrate to reduce the risk of ever encountering a disturbing number of spurned, nutcase hotties.

The final episode of *The Bachelor* was preceded by a one-hour program in which the twenty-three women who had already been sent packing were afforded the opportunity to speak out. Alex, meanwhile, brought the two finalists home to meet Mom and Dad. "I think there is some fear on the part of my family that I'm ruining my life," Alex confessed to the camera.

Of course there was, Alex. That's why we were watching.

8. Looking for Love: Bachelorettes in Alaska (Fox),

June 9, 2002

Looking for Love: Bachelorettes in Alaska opened with a shot of the female contestants, each dolled up in a fashionable bridal gown, trudging up a snow-covered mountain. "Five single women have journeyed to Alaska, desperately seeking husbands," the show's host intoned in solemn voice-over. "Here, plenty of eligible bachelors are eager to find wives." The sequence was but a haunting flute solo away from a "Hinterland Who's Who" vignette, those ancient, minute-long, government-crafted glimpses into the fascinating world of Canadian wildlife: *The Alaskan bachelor hibernates in snowy climes. But when mating season begins, this feisty male is prepared to go to astonishing lengths – even willingly demean himself on national television! – in his single-minded quest to get some.*

Here's the show in a nutshell (and believe me, it would fit): Five single women. A bunch of single men. An assortment of outdoorsy "dates." An obligatory weekly trip to the Jacuzzi so that Fox executives wouldn't lapse into cardiac arrest over the surfeit of parkas and dearth of bikinis. And terrible, terrible poetry. "Your legs," Jack recited in an effort to win the heart of Rebekah, "are as long and graceful as a deer prancing through the meadow." And really, what woman doesn't adore being compared to a cloven-hoofed, four-legged ruminant?

At the end of each show, the women donned white boots, white pants, a white jacket, a white turtleneck, and a white furry hat and – looking for all the world as though they were fleeing servitude as members of the Michelin Man's harem – trekked to Proposal Point, where they were tortured with crude expressions of manly affection. In the final episode, each woman waited at Promise Lake to see if her man would come to propose marriage. In the meantime, everyone spent a lot of time hanging around Cape Humiliation.

Bachelorettes in Alaska was awful, which was not unexpected, but it was not awful in a good and entertaining way, and that was a surprise. Part of the problem was a fundamental misunderstanding about what the audience wants in a "romantic" reality show. The people who conceived and edited this series went to great lengths to embarrass the participants. When, for instance, four new bachelors entered the game in one episode, they were each obliged to attempt to catch upwards of twenty large salmon that were hurled at them from a not-insignificant distance. The guy who snagged the most fish got first pick of the ladies and, presumably, first dibs on the laundry facilities.

Here's what the creators didn't get: mocking and ridiculing the participants on a reality show is our job. It's what we in the television audience do. That's why *The Bachelor* was such an unanticipated success: it took the proceedings seriously, it played up the drama and the emotion, it portrayed the players as sincere, and spared no expense in depositing them in glamorous settings. We believed that they believed a marriage might actually come of it. And those of us who watched sat and cringed and sneered and needled and otherwise thoroughly enjoyed ourselves.

This Fox series, by comparison, deprived us of our supporting role. No small number of the men were freaks, some of them in a cute and eccentric way, such as poor, chubby Michael. None of the women wanted to date him, even though his expectations were depressingly low ("I'm a sucker for a smooth pair of legs," he informed us. Not a great pair. Not a long pair or a shapely pair. Just a smooth pair. Things are apparently tougher up there than even Fox led us to believe).

Others, however, were freaks of a more, well, freaky sort, such as Patrick, who attempted to impress his date by belching with frequency and vigour. It's as though a casting director ordered scouts to fan out across the state and approach anyone with peculiar social tendencies: "Think hermit!" she must have decreed. "Think Unabomber, but without the whole hair thing!"

Eventually, Michael was paired with a bachelorette on a pity date. The most handsome guy got to take his gal to a spa; Michael was ordered to go fishing. He didn't have much luck with the fish or with the lady. Trying to charm his companion with self-deprecating humour, at one point he inquired, "Can fish smell desperation?" No, but women can. And so, much to the chagrin of Fox, could most television viewers.

9. Celebrity Fear Factor (NBC), September 23, 2002

A tough day for Gena Lee Nolin. The *Baywatch* alumna was required to sit inside a car that was crushed by the monster truck Bigfoot and to frolic in a tank of water occupied by 1,001 snakes. Later, she was offered a tasty snack of Madagascar hissing cockroach. So it is really saying something that, from all visual evidence, the most objectionable aspect of the competition was enduring the groping embrace of Greg Brady.

Barry Williams, who played the eldest Brady boy for five years before beginning a successful career in reminding people that he played the eldest Brady boy for five years, was among the "celebrities" enlisted for this ninety-minute prime-time special. After injuring nothing more than the stray remnants of his dignity during his encounter with Bigfoot, Williams lumbered over to the not-unattractive Nolin and inquired in sucky-baby kidspeak, "Hug from Gena Lee?" She obliged, but with a look that could plausibly lead the Madagascar hissing cockroach to conclude that, by comparison, it had a pretty decent shot at hooking up with her.

In one year alone, I saw Williams on *The Weakest Link*, *Celebrity Boxing*, and *Fear Factor*, an achievement that must hearten all former child stars out there, who can think to themselves, "Well, at least I haven't hit rock bottom." (Warning: "Heartening" may not occur in cases involving former child stars whose name includes the words "Todd" and "Bridges.")

10. The Bachelor, season two, episode one,

September 25, 2002

The promos for the second season of *The Bachelor* were such a tease. They showed fleeting glimpses of the man: an arm here, some gleaming teeth there, a brow furrowed in manly cerebration. On repeated viewing, the spots gave the impression that Bachelor 2.0 had been constructed in the manner of Frankenstein's monster: the abs of an underwear model, the nose of soap star, the wry smile of a man who'd been trapped for days in the cleavage of Heather Graham. I could almost hear his infantile utterance: "Women. Good. More women. Gooder."

The first episode turned out to be a tease, too, a chronicle of how producers sifted through the rednecks ("I can't find any wimmin here who enjoy the huntin' and the fishin'," one lamented in his video submission), the misogynists, the horn-dogs, the megalomaniacs, the perverts, and one creepy, creepy old guy to decide who they would present with an all-new harem of twenty-five desperate, unchoosy women. The rest of the gentlemen would, presumably, have their lascivious applications automatically forwarded to local law-enforcement officials, or, more likely, to the producers of *Blind Date*.

"Since the last show ended," host Chris Harrison said, "I've been bombarded with questions from fans across the country!" Who is the new Bachelor? Are Alex and Amanda (the couple that emerged from the first instalment of *The Bachelor*) still together? To whom do I direct queries regarding the prompt and unconditional return of the six hours of my life I wasted watching your debasing slutfest? That sort of thing.

If it weren't so thoroughly coated in a thick, gooey patina of abject sleaze, the episode might almost have been touching in its depiction of human desperation. It presented an almost ceaseless montage of overly groomed fellas unconvincingly proclaiming their hunky, heterosexual cred ("I am truly blessed that women do find me sexy in almost every capacity") and anxious ladies describing a profound weariness with the singles scene ("I want a ring on this finger *now!*"). To watch these women auditioning to become a prime-time floozie, to see them forced to get up and dance for the benefit of show's stern, humourless producers – well, for me, it pretty much took the "y pleasure" out of this "guilty pleasure."

In the end, Bachelor 2.0 was identified as Aaron, a twenty-eight-year-old vice-president of a small bank in Missouri. He was pictured shirtless a great deal, doubtless to show off his "sincerity," which Robinson claimed was the attribute that producers had deemed most important. To be fair, his abs seemed very sincere. As did Amanda, by the way, who said (a) she's still dating Alex (though they live in different cities) and (b) that Alex. Is. Not. Gay. She also passed along to Bachelor 2.0, by way of friendly advice, that "maybe it's not necessary to stick your tongue down every girl's throat."

It might not be necessary. But that doesn't make it any less likely.

11. The Bachelor, season two, episode two, October 2, 2002
As the twenty-five contestants sashayed past Bachelor 2.0, a soft-focus blur of shiny lips and buoyant cleavage, we checked off each "type" against the handy "Bachelor Program Guide" that we'd received in the current edition of *Trolloping Monthly*: "There's the Virgin," we'd yell. Or, "There's the Beauty Queen!" Or, "Run, Aaron, run for your life: there's the Scary, Scary One!" (Quoth the Scary One: "I am twenty-four years old. I want to be married by twenty-six. I want to have two babies by the time I'm thirty.") The only trouble we had was differentiating the Woman Who Makes Bad Decisions from the Woman Who Makes Even Worse Decisions. All we knew was that one of them was Camille, who told us, "It seems like I meet the same type of guys, who, within the first few days

are talking about, 'So you ever been with another woman? You into threesomes?' "

Aaron was an immediately likeable fellow who looked not unlike Ben Affleck, but whose facial expressions are more Matt Damon: not an unpleasing combination, judging from the ladies' reaction (bulging eyeballs, flushed cheeks, copious use of the word "hottie"). And when Bachelor 2.0 sat down and played the piano, thus revealing his sensitive side – well, it was all these women could do to refrain from shucking their clingy gowns and crushing their prey in a great big floozie pile-on. Later, as he roamed the room, Aaron told us the experience of socializing with twenty-five attractive strumpets was, all things considered, "just like any other date," a statement that, if nothing else, seemed sure to prompt a tourism boom in his little corner of Missouri.

The Bachelor soon had me in its skanky clutches, not least because it had established itself as the only show on which you can see an attractive woman, upon departing for the beach on a group date with the Bachelor, stare into the camera and declare with a look of genuine consternation, "Usually, when I'm on a date with someone, I don't bring my two hottest friends and their boobs."

Still, something was missing. Could it have been the passion? The emotion? The on-site presence of the herpes containment unit of the Centers for Disease Control? All I know is that the women were neither catty nor loose enough, the Bachelor was neither unscrupulous nor grabby enough, and the outcome each week was neither unpredictable nor tearful enough. I don't want to talk crazy here, but it's almost as though these were real, actual people looking for, I don't know, love or something. I mean, one week I almost had . . . geez, I'm embarrassed even to admit it . . . I almost had a Sympathetic Feeling. Don't get me wrong – I suppressed it. I beat it into submission by recalling the peerlessly slutty exploits of Amanda in *The Bachelor I*. But, like, *whew*. That was close.

This is not to say the show was entirely without demerit. During one segment, for instance, Aaron went on solo dates with the three women – of the six that remained – who were judged most compatible with him by virtue of a "scientifically designed" personality analysis. This actually marked the second aspect of the show that was "scientifically designed," the first being the breasts of at least four of the contestants.

In any event, the computer (apparently a VIC-20) decreed that Heather, thirty years old and from Texas, was, despite all evidence to the contrary, a primo match for Aaron. She spent the entire date caressing his pecs and cooing about how much chemistry there was between them. Aaron, meanwhile, sported the grimacing visage of a man enduring a four-hour colonoscopy. "I didn't really feel anything," Aaron told us later, though few viewers believed him. After all, there's just no way he could have missed feeling Heather's foot lurking about in the general vicinity of his crotch.

12. The Bachelor/The Victoria's Secret Fashion Show
(ABC & CBS), November 20, 2002

I have a weakness for television's baser, more ignoble creations: your *Bachelor*s, your *Temptation Island*s, your *Dog Eats Dog*s. There could be a profound, compelling reason for this – a rogue element of my psyche that defines me as a deeply flawed monster who delights in the misery and misfortune of others. Or maybe I just like women's breasts.

Either way, I'd looked forward to this evening the way a prison lifer looks forward to the "How to Fashion a Shiv from Your Bunion" edition of craft night. Using my satellite receiver, I'd even discovered a way to watch the first hour of the finale of *The Bachelor*, then switch to *The Victoria's Secret Fashion Show*, and finally tune to the last hour of *The Bachelor*. I was as happy as a pig in a place that was not devoted to the slaughter and processing of pigs.

Alas, *The Bachelor* began in Dullsville, and then drove on through Borington and the Doldrums before arriving in the capital of reality-show hell, New Tedium. Aaron had reduced his harem of twenty-five unchoosy, and in some cases criminally insane, women to two: Helene, a twenty-seven-year-old school psychologist from New Jersey, and Brooke, a twenty-two-year-old halfwit. Our Bachelor dutifully took each lady home to meet the folks, both of whom turned out to be perfectly nice people, not at all confrontational or judgemental – qualities that are to be admired, except of course on prime-time TV, where they're about as interesting as what Rosie O'Donnell *really* thinks about important social issues.

The only indelible moment from the first hour came when Brooke was asked which final two classes she required to obtain her college degree. Her reply: "Golf. And Volleyball." You see, Brooke was at school in Alabama, which means she must have already aced the course prerequisites: Walking Upright and Finding the Campus.

The Victoria's Secret Fashion Show began at nine, thus ensuring that countless fathers and young boys would be able to bond with a tender, heartfelt dialogue about whether Gisele or Heidi has the superior rack. The show was preceded by a warning that the program would contain "mature subject matter." Or, as we in the trade refer to it, "asses." Small, naked asses trembling with thongly indignation. "Thousands try out, but only a few are selected!" we were informed, and for the rest of the hour I could not stop thinking about how it must feel to earn your living assessing women's rumps and declaring, "Sorry, sweetheart, that fanny doesn't cut it. It's just not *a Victoria's Secret ass*!"

The fashion show itself – sandwiched between live performances of a trio of cruddy pop songs and the mood-killing ignominy of Heidi Klum actually opening her mouth and talking – consisted of a seemingly endless parade of scantily clad women marching angrily down the runway, sneerily posing, and then abruptly turning and stomping away, like hookers who'd been asked if they accept postdated cheques. At one point, Tyra Banks interrupted the monotonous procession by performing a flamenco dance. Or perhaps she was suffering a violent seizure. Either way, very jiggly.

It was, by my calculations, forty-three minutes into the broadcast before a model dared to smile; she was a blonde, if I recall correctly. I remember her stopping, smiling, twirling, and then returning backstage, where she was presumably bludgeoned to death in a hail of fury and blood-soaked Manolo Blahniks. Meantime, the show went on, and we glimpsed yet more hot chicks adorned in feathers, gigantic novelty wings, and thongs so snug that their butt cheeks seemed as violently cleaved as the former Yugoslavia. The proceedings came to a suitably absurd end with the arrival of the "Victoria's Secret flying angels," which descended from high above, like so many fluttering, earthbound trollops.

Similarly, the final hour of *The Bachelor* was devoid of intrigue, and I found myself writing down quotes from the commercials, which were far more interesting ("Genital herpes used to get me down!" began one, which I think was for a drug of some sort. Or maybe Dennis Rodman was marketing a self-help book). As decision day approached, Aaron confessed it was "very difficult to stay focused." He said he was "finding it all really difficult." And he confirmed that "it's going to be tough to let one woman go." Such heartbreak! And with Utah so tantalizingly nearby!

When the end came, you could have cut through the tension with a Fisher-Price spoon. "I'm not 100 per cent convinced we're at the same point in our lives," Aaron advised Brooke. For instance, I'm a rich guy who's about to be happily married to someone else. And you've got volleyball class! Brooke seemed to take it okay, but later went all wiggy in the obligatory Dramatic Post-Dumping Interview. "I should have said, 'You just made the biggest mistake of your life!'" she blubbered, bawling as though she'd just missed a birdie putt that would have given her an A+. "I don't understand what the hell's going on!" Brooke summed it all up by saying her "heart is smashed into a thousand pieces," but that "it was worth it." With that utterance, the registration computer at Brooke's college crashed from the flood of horny young men attempting to enroll in Golf and Volleyball.

Later, when Aaron finally popped the question, enthusing in a dreamy voice-over that the sight of Helene on that very day had, in his eyes, "sealed our fate together." Not exactly a Hallmark sentiment, unless you're browsing the company's new Utterly Doomed to a Painful Death line of greeting cards. Nevertheless, an appropriate image on which to end the night. Aaron and Helene and all the rest of us were in this mess together. We were with them for better and, on this evening, for much, much worse.

Note: Aaron and Helene broke up shortly after the series was aired. Naturally, ABC made a prime-time special out of that, too.

13. Celebrity Boot Camp (Fox), September 30, 2002

It was shortly after the United States Marine Corps drill instructors had shaved off Coolio's moustache – right around the time that one instructor made Barry Williams sing aloud a song he had written entitled "The Real Greg Brady," and another inquired of David Faustino (the guy who played Al Bundy's stupid, horny son on *Married . . . With Children*), "Bud Bundy, right? You gotta be kiddin' me. Do you actually *tell* people that?" – that I began to think that Fox's *Celebrity Boot Camp* just might be one of the funniest shows ever produced for television.

I am, it is perhaps redundant to mention at this point, not picky about where I acquire my yuks. A pithy Shakespearean jest, the sight of a trio of drill instructors propelling copious saliva onto the dazed visage of Kato Kaelin, it's all the same to me. And by that impossibly low standard, *Celebrity Boot Camp* notched more bursts of genuine (and often reluctant) laughter than the drollest *Frasier*, the wittiest *Seinfeld*, or the most arrested former child star.

The two-hour special employed a similar format, and used the same stentorian drill instructors, as the reality series *Boot Camp*, which had aired to unenthusiastic ratings the previous season. And so there were physical and mental challenges, a process by which "recruits" were eliminated, and a fifty-thousand-dollar cash prize. There was also an awful lot of free-ranging spittle and the nagging sense that if Saddam Hussein were somehow watching, he'd have ordered the prompt decommissioning of all weapons of mass destruction – anything to keep his country free from the unspeakable horror of a Marine assault that might include a tuneless, crooning Greg Brady.

The show was populated, for the most part, by "celebrities" who were not quite famous enough to make the cut for

Celebrity Boxing: former pop tart Tiffany, soon-to-be-former pop tart Vitamin C, Lorenzo Lamas, That One Guy from Milli Vanilli Who's Not Dead, Some Chick from *The Price Is Right* Who Posed for *Playboy*, and, in the other curiously snug half-shirt, Some Chick from *Baywatch* Who Posed for *Playboy*.

And then there was Kato. Poor, sad Kato. Kato, who achieved a peculiar, septic celebrity as O.J. Simpson's clueless house guest. Kato, who was unable to perform the taxing chore of counting off to four during a recruit march. Kato, who bellyached that the prescribed thirty-second urination interval was insufficient because it takes him "like, fifteen minutes" to negotiate entry into his pants. Kato, who, given the reward of a one-minute call, rushed into the bunker to phone his daughter, dialled a wrong number, and proceeded to waste his precious minute by leaving a surreal, detailed message from Recruit Kaelin on the answering machine of someone he had never met. "He dials the wrong number," a drill instructor explained to the camera by way of summing up, "and you just kinda want to go" – at this point, the instructor waved his hand in front of his face in the manner of trying to snap someone out of a trance – "you want to go, 'Is there anybody home?'"

It will not startle you, surely, to learn that Kato did not win the loot. Nor did the Bud Bundy guy, who was overwhelmed by the rigorous challenge of making his bed. Meantime, under orders not to provide an enemy interrogator with any strategic information, Traci Bingham (the *Baywatch*/*Playboy* hottie, for those of you scoring hotties at home) technically obeyed the command by providing the foe with *all* the strategic information, except for this valuable little tidbit that she saved to for our ears alone: "What I can't wait for," she told us, remarking coyly on the workout she was getting at *Boot Camp*, "is to strip out of this uniform and just look at myself nude in the mirror."

And then there was Coolio, the tough-as-nails rapper, who demonstrated his irascible bad-boy cred and detestation of authority by . . . trying to smuggle a muffin out of the mess hall. Later, he lamented that his forced shave had left him with what he called "booty face." As if somehow sensing the confusion descending over the homes of millions of white people, Coolio elaborated: "No moustache. And I got big lips, too. Big lips and no moustache. That's not cool." So we had a rap performer worrying about how an absence of facial hair might damage his street cred. As he appeared on a reality-TV show. With Greg Brady. It was the most hilarious thing I'd seen for a long while, at least until a dismissed Greg Brady returned to help decide the winner of *Celebrity Boot Camp* and uttered the phrase, "Therefore, I pledge my dog tags to Recruit Coolio."

An infinite number of scholars pensively rubbing an infinite number of bearded chins could not in a million years concoct a more cogent or efficient representation of the peculiar phenomenon of modern celebrity. A former child star, who decades later still sings about the role that made him (in)famous. An ex-con rapper reduced to bootlegging muffins and lamenting his bare upper lip on national television. It's a good thing the show was so funny, because otherwise it would have been really sad.

14. Joe Millionaire (Fox), January 13, 2003

TV viewers are all such liars! Their mouths say, "Reality TV is so tedious and passé." But their clicker thumbs say, "Hey, those greedy babes think that dopey lunkhead is loaded! Let's watch!"

Joe Millionaire was the dupe du jour. The novel gimmick of the series was that its obligatory gimmick was a lie. Twenty young ladies were told that a dark, hulking, and – how shall I put this? – not intellectually intimidating American chap named Evan had recently inherited fifty million dollars, a revelation that brought about much feminine shrieking and indecorous hopping about, not to mention the prospect of a copyright-infringement suit from the producers of *Looney Tunes* over the cartoon dollar signs that appeared on the ladies' eyeballs. But as we were informed from the outset, Evan was in fact a construction worker from California who earned just nineteen thousand dollars a year. When this average Joe ultimately came clean to the contestant he'd selected, I'm guessing it served as small comfort to the woman that, as a bulldozer operator, he could really make the earth move for her.

The show was set at a palatial French château (or is it a châteauial French palace?) and had so far been memorable primarily for the fact that, even by reality-series standards, very little happened. There was a tedious bit of ballroom dancing, uneventful group dates (not even a grope!), and a bunch of shots in which, judging by his pained grimace, Evan was either horribly conflicted about living this lie or trying to remember his own phone number. "The more I think about it," he said in sombre voice-over, "the more it eats my brain out." Alas, I fear this wouldn't had made for much of a meal.

After the solemn faux romanticism of *The Bachelor*, a show that was rife with such gooey prattle as "making an intimate connection" and "finding a soulmate," there was no small amount of allure in hearing Evan on his rationale for keeping certain women in the game. Of the blonde, attractive Sarah, for instance, Evan was heard to rhapsodize, "She's a little more uptight than the other girls, but she's hot, so I'm going to give her a shot." And let me assure you, no aficionado of poetry will soon forget this rapturous couplet, composed on the subject of Alison: "She's got the red hair, the red pants. She's red hot, she's on fire."

The highlight of one episode was the expulsion from the château of, among others, Heidi, the charmless, twenty-four-year-old businesswoman who put the "bitch" in "What a bitch!" Heidi's first transgression was to enter a room where twenty dresses had been put out for the twenty women and immediately grab *two* gowns. "Hey, you can't do that!" I actually hollered. Then she went and spoiled a day's horseback riding by crying and turning back after proclaiming, "I have a fear of being on something I can't control." (Apparently, she reckoned Evan would be safer to mount.) Finally, she admitted to the other girls that she had a boyfriend back home. If looks could kill, Evan and the gals would have been obliged to embark on a fourth group date: an evening's gravedigging.

Joe Millionaire was probably evil and it was definitely mean-spirited. But after almost three years of hokey tribal councils and absurdly melodramatic rose ceremonies, after almost three years of wondering why anyone would subject herself to the demeaning reality-TV experience, it was a kick to watch these naive, shallow participants being played for naive and, well, shallow. And for fools, above all.

15. Married by America (Fox), March 31, 2003
Not many people watched *Married by America*, an unexpected development that raised a deep and perplexing philosophical question: If a loose woman surrenders herself to a studly mandroid on international television and no one tunes in to see it, does she still contract gonorrhea?

Some television critics interpreted the ratings of this and other reality series from the spring of 2003 as evidence that viewers, after tuning in en masse to *Joe Millionaire*, had abruptly sprouted a healthy growth of good sense. This theory could not be ruled out, although the ongoing popularity of the charmless sitcom *According to Jim* served as a persuasive counterpoint. More likely, it was a byproduct of bad timing. After watching *Joe Millionaire* and *The Bachelorette*, we'd all grown weary of suppressing the urge to reach through the television screen and crisply thwack dimwitted reality-show contestants with a rolled-up newspaper.

Perhaps the best way to convey the experience of watching *Married by America*, short of coming to your home and setting fire to your brain, is to describe what happened during the episode in which Kevin and Jill – who earlier in the series were matched up by well-meaning American TV viewers – went to visit Jill's parents on Long Island. Ominously, Jill warned us, "My family is dysfunctional with a capital D!"

Kevin's parents showed up, too – a surprise! – and the party was on. You could tell it was a party because there was food and loud conversation and because Jill's father, Tony, kept taking off his shirt to reveal his thick, broadloom back hair. Tony was confrontational, coarse, and, when he ventured outside, prone to wearing a light spring jacket with no shirt underneath. The whole of his screen time resembled a series of outtakes from *My Cousin Vinny*.

Tony, we quickly came to understand, was of a mind that ten days of furious televised fondling was, when it came to his little angel, an insufficient courtship. He forced Kevin to sleep in a guest room. He treated him with swaggering hostility. And then, during the party, when he overheard Kevin innocently address Jill as "sweetie," Tony snapped.

"Don't call her 'sweetie'!" he hollered. "Don't do it!" Jill's mother tried to calm Tony down, but words failed where only a well-placed tranquilizer dart or an anvil to the head could have succeeded. "Whose roof is this?" Tony bellowed. "He's Kevin! She's Jill! Enough with this 'sweetie' shit!" And then to Kevin: "Don't get me pissed off!" Eventually, Tony fell glumly silent, which allowed Jill to continue a heated debate with Kevin's parents, who had denounced her plans to pose again for *Playboy*. In-laws: is there anything they don't disapprove of?

The following morning, Kevin, doubtless after confirming that his dental insurance was in order, approached Tony and delicately asked for permission to marry his daughter. I found myself wondering: Will Fox show the evisceration, or just allude to it? But Tony, the effects of his exposure to a bombardment of gamma rays having apparently passed for the moment, pondered it briefly and replied, "I'm gonna give you a shot. I'm gonna give you my blessing. All right, son?"

THE BACHELOR:
BACHELORETTE APPLICATION FORM

(Please print clearly, especially if using crayon)

Name: _____

Age: _____

Nickname *(if any)*: _____

Did you decline to enter an answer above because your nick-name is not "Any"?   YES

Measurements: _____

(If first number exceeds 38, please send photo for confirmation. Come to think of it, send a bunch of photos. If second or third number exceeds 38, send photos into small, intense blaze ignited at bottom of metallic garbage can.)

1. Do you believe in love at first sight? *(Circle one)*   YES NO

2. Do you believe in demeaning yourself at the first sight of an unattached man and a television camera? *(Circle yes)*   YES

3. What is the ratio of your IQ to your shoe size:

_____ 10:1

_____ 5:1

_____ 1:1

_____ Wait, I'm still counting my toes!

149

4. On a scale of 1 to 10, how would you rate your level of self-esteem? *(To help speed the application process, we have already inserted the minus sign required to denote a negative integer.)*

–
‒‒‒‒‒‒‒‒

5a. Describe your most embarrassing moment:

‒‒‒

5b. Assuming you are selected to participate, describe how you would feel about that embarrassing moment becoming your second-most embarrassing moment:

‒‒‒

6. Number of *Garfield* cartoons currently attached to your refrigerator by novelty magnets:

‒‒‒‒‒‒‒ 25-30

‒‒‒‒‒‒‒ 31-40

‒‒‒‒‒‒‒ Way more! That Odie is *such* a cutie!

7a. In which of the following ways have you attempted to find your potential soulmate? *(Check all that apply)*

‒‒‒‒‒‒‒ Club scene

‒‒‒‒‒‒‒ Internet chat rooms

‒‒‒‒‒‒‒ Determined stalking of anywhere from three to seven Baldwin brothers

‒‒‒‒‒‒‒ Dr. Frankenstein–type perverting of God's great plan

‒‒‒‒‒‒‒ Working tirelessly to "convert" known homosexuals

‒‒‒‒‒‒‒ Fashioning own "perfect man" from crude amalgam of straw, gum, and burlap

_____ Revealing left breast to nerd from accounting after chugging four Singapore slings at office Christmas party

_____ Blind dates

7b. Which of the following words were said to you by a man as he attempted to break up with you after a brief relationship? *(Check all)*

_____ Need more space

_____ Too clingy

_____ High-maintenance

_____ Moody

_____ Don't cry

_____ Why are you crying?

_____ Don't yell at me, freak girl!

_____ Knife-wielding wacko

_____ Are you crazy? Don't jab that thing at me!

_____ Ow!

_____ Jesus, are you completely insane?

_____ Aiiieeeee!

8. Why do you want to be on *The Bachelor*? *(Check only the third one)*

_____ Sounds like good, innocent fun

_____ Willing to try anything to meet ideal mate

_____ Recent foray into hardcore porn did not result in expected level of public humiliation

9. In ten words or fewer, describe your best attributes. *(Please limit yourself to four uses of the word "knockers.")*

10. Some commentators are bound to suggest that women who appear on *The Bachelor* are whores. How would you respond to these allegations? *(Check one)*

———— These taunts are profoundly archaic: I prefer to be addressed as a ho.

———— It makes me so mad when they do that! So I usually end up charging them double.

———— How can I be a whore if I give it away for free?

11. Complete the following three sentences by circling one of the choices:

i. A stitch in time saves:

     a) nine.

     b) Who the hell cares? I need a man!

ii. My breasts are:

     a) big.

     b) really big.

     c) right here, big boy . . . oh, wait, you're supposed to buy me a drink before I show you those.

iii. When I look at myself in the mirror, I see:

     a) an attractive, appealing woman who will eventually be a perfect wife to some lucky man.

b) an insecure person who has a lot to offer but is struggling to find love in this crazy world.

c) nothing. I see nothing at all. I am invisible to the world.

Note: If you checked (c), you are emotionally damaged and in desperate need of intensive psychiatric help. Or you might be a vampire. Either way, you're in!

12. Should you be rejected by our Bachelor, your pathetic onscreen desperation will nevertheless result in much attention being paid to you by a vast array of creepy, low-life fetishists and devious, cagey users of easy women. Do you want us to provide these men with your home phone or cellphone number? *(Circle one)*   BOTH!

13a. What do you look for in a man? *(Check all that apply)*

_____ Hunky looks

_____ Intelligence

_____ Courage

_____ Sense of humour

_____ Cultural sophistication

13b. What are you willing to settle for in a man? *(Check all)*

_____ Pulse

_____ Not less than one and not more than four limbs

_____ Er . . . that's it.

_____ Wait! I'm flexible on the limb thing!

14. Have you been treated for any mental illness(es) in the last ten (10) years? YES NO

If NO, please attach a separate sheet of paper detailing precisely why you think being on our show is a good idea. Seriously, we're curious.

Disclaimer: By submitting this application, I hereby consent to the recording, use, reuse, and shameless manipulation for purposes of portraying me as a one-dimensional manipulative bitch-goddess of my voice, actions, likeness, name, and appearance. I further agree that the American Broadcasting Company may use my likeness in connection with any and all promotion, publicity, marketing, or advertisement, even if said usage makes folks back home look at me funny when I get on the bus.

Signature: _____

Date: _____

You! Are! Next!

A chance encounter, some time in the future, between two members of the cast of the original Survivor.

COLLEEN: Sean, how are you?!

SEAN: Wow, Colleen! I'm good, I'm good. Well, mostly good – I lost my licence to do that whole neurosurgeon thing. I don't know what it was, but I could just never remember which side of the body the brain is on.

COLLEEN: Um, isn't that, like, the thing in your head . . . well, not in *your* head, but in heads in general?

SEAN: So *that's* why patients kept asking me to explain those scars on their abdomen!

COLLEEN: You kind of, like, disappeared after getting all those showbiz gigs when the show ended. What happened?

SEAN: Well, I was doing really well as a medical correspondent for that TV show *Extra*, but then they started getting mail saying I was mixing up things on the air – you know, "cerebrum" instead of the more accurate "cerebellum," or, like that one time, saying "eat as much of the stuff as you want" instead of the more accurate "place it in the vicinity of your lips and you'll die."

COLLEEN: Oh yeah, I remember that. Have you and Susan spoken since her husband's funeral?

SEAN: Not really. I saw her not long ago, and I tried to explain that any medical professional could mistake a horribly lethal plant for a tasty chocolatey confection, but I could tell she wasn't ready to talk about it yet by the look in her eyes . . . and by the way she pounded on the visitors'-room glass and shouted, "When I get out of here for beating the crap out of that scheming, backstabbing, bare-arsed Rich, you're next, moron. You! Are! Next!"

COLLEEN: But isn't she going to be released soon on parole? I remember the judge cited all those mitigating circumstances, like "someone was bound to do it" and "he pretty much deserved it" and "man, that porker was a complete jackass."

SEAN: Yeah, but I'm not worried. I've always had a good way with people and an ability to make them like and trust me. Except, you know, the ones who own televisions . . .

COLLEEN: Yeah.

SEAN: . . . or who know people that do (sighs wearily). So what's new with you? Seen anyone else from the show lately?

COLLEEN: Gervase is good. He had so many children with so many women that the New York Knicks gave him a tryout. And I saw Rudy not long ago browsing in a paint store with his partner, Rex.

SEAN: His partner?

COLLEEN: You didn't know? Rudy was gay all along. After the reunion show I, like, saw him pinch Rich's butt and giggle back-stage, and he saw me see him, and he kind of looked at me, like, sheepishly and said, "What? You never saw *American Beauty*?"

SEAN: Wow. I did not see that one coming at all. Then again, I also failed to foresee that Jenna would win all those daytime Emmys or that Rich would make a mint with his "Satan and Me" workshops. You know, the whole "success through an eternity of blind servitude" thing. And I certainly didn't expect that Nokia would pay a huge amount to buy that Nature Phone idea off Greg.

COLLEEN: Um, yeah, about that – that's just the story that Greg's family told him. The Nokia people got so frightened of Greg that he's never allowed back into Finland again. His sister just slices open a fresh coconut each morning, sticks a Nokia logo on the shell, and attaches it to Greg's belt. He hasn't noticed the difference.

SEAN (*looking down at his waist*): Damn! You mean this one he sold me doesn't work?

INTERNAL MEMORANDUM

From: Mark Burnett, Executive Producer, *Survivor*
Subject: *Celebrity Survivor*

My thanks to all of you who've been working to lay the groundwork for the most anticipated *Survivor* yet: *Celebrity Survivor*! I am delighted to be able to announce officially that CBS has at last given its formal blessing to begin production, with the intention of airing the first few episodes during May Sweeps. I don't think I'm exaggerating when I say this instalment has the potential to produce our highest ratings since the finale of *Survivor: Macy's on the Day After Thanksgiving*, when, tragically, our four remaining contestants were trampled into unconsciousness during a stampede set off by the unexpected arrival at the store of Jennifer Lopez. Even now, more than a year later, I find myself lying in bed at night, picturing the scene, remembering J.Lo's arrival and asking myself: Why was everyone so eager to get away from her?

Alas, there are no answers. Well, there's her latest record, I suppose (*Jenny Bought the Block and Had It Razed to Build Luxury Condos*). That could have set it off. Or maybe it was the boorish manner in which she left her (would-be) seventh husband, Larry King, standing at the altar two weeks earlier –

a fact that would have been of only trivial consequence if millions hadn't already forked out $49.95 to watch the wedding ceremony on pay-per-view.

Whatever the case, this unpleasantness is in the past, and the time has come for those of us in the *Survivor* family to get back to work. The purpose of this memo is to spur along the pre-production process and ensure that everyone is brought up to speed on where we stand right now in terms of (a) locations, (b) casting, and (c) furthering the sense of moral decay that has come to dominate the medium of television (ha ha – that's a joke. We'll leave that to *Fear Factor* and *Meet the Press*). First, the nuts and bolts. Our sixteen celebrity Survivors will be divided into two tribes: Guttenberg (from the German, meaning "fleeting career success") and Bonaduce (from the Italian, meaning "irresistibly cute until age twelve.") Each tribe will be given a small supply of provisions – just the staples required for basic celebrity sustenance (water, botox, a sycophantic hanger-on) – and abandoned in the middle of nowhere with only their wits, their physical strength, and roughly 275 camera operators, sound technicians, Teamsters, and support staff.

This seems a good time to stress something that is of fundamental importance: *Celebrity Survivor* will cease to make for compelling television at the precise moment we confer upon these contestants any sort of preferential treatment. Yes, we will be documenting a competition among the wealthy and famous. And yes, our celebrities are quite accustomed to being doted upon, being catered to, being fawned over. But we cannot allow our viewers to sense that these would-be Survivors are having an easy go of it. Sadly, I've already had to fire one production assistant for agreeing to act as a hoagie mule for Dom DeLuise.

That aside, I've been quite impressed with other aspects of our preparatory work, especially the planning team's list of potential immunity and reward challenges. These will be difficult and demanding and, just as important, very entertaining. Don't want to spill all the beans just yet, but . . . in place of standing for hours upon a beam, our endurance challenge will consist of a far more gruelling ordeal: a Dan Aykroyd Film Festival. Yes, even *Celtic Pride*. I can hear the screams of agony already! (I mean that literally: the prep team's office is down the hall and I'm forcing them to watch *Blues Brothers 2000*.) And later, as the stakes get even higher, the remaining Survivors will be subjected to one of the harshest tests of their character: stripped of their aides, their valets, and even their posse, the members of the competing tribes will be forced to dress themselves. Note to the network: Just speculating here, but we may need to make that a two-hour special.

So, splendid work all around, people. The only challenge I'm concerned about is the Paparazzi Smackdown. Don't get me wrong: I adore the trying physical aspects of the challenge. And I certainly have no moral or philosophical objection to our Survivors being obliged to single-handedly chase, corral, and ruthlessly bloody a tabloid photographer, all while holding a newborn baby. It works both as a savagely primitive exercise and as devastating social commentary. But just a thought: Doesn't this confer too great a competitive advantage on Alec Baldwin?

Speaking of casting, I am delighted to report that Calista Flockhart is in. True, she said no originally, but word is she's up for a couple of big movie roles – real character stuff, like Zellweger in *Bridget Jones* – and she figures that eating two small helpings of rice each day would be a good way to gain some weight. Robert De Niro is also confirmed. That's right, *the* Robert De Niro. Frankly, I don't quite know how we convinced him to do it, either, but somehow he had just enough time between finishing production on *Raging Bull 2: Still Raging!* and starting work as the new pitchman for Miller Lite. On a sadder note, I've had to turn down Charlie Sheen. I know it's disappointing: he's a charismatic actor who would have brought a welcome levity to the proceedings. But I concluded it simply wasn't within the spirit of the rules that he be able to bring as his luxury item a buxom call girl who has several bottles of rum taped to her thighs. Melanie Griffith, meanwhile, has expressed interest, but I'm going to have to check with our Legal Standards Branch on this one: I want to be certain she still officially qualifies as a celebrity.

I'm sure that by now many of you have seen the correspondence from Cher's attorneys. I responded in as sympathetic a manner as possible, but I did not waver from our previously expressed view that the torches of tribal council are an integral component of the *Survivor* experience and cannot be abandoned or altered, no matter how great the risk that they might warp or melt certain "non-indigenous" components of her physique. Do I want Cher to be a participant on *Celebrity Survivor*? I most certainly do. But it has to be on our terms. Here's where we've left it: she has an appointment next week at the local Subaru dealership to have a thick layer of protective "clear-coat" applied. Apparently, it will prevent any heat-related damage while at the same time enhancing the resale value of her cheekbones.

With Andy Dick, alas, I had to be more stern. I understand the health-related issues he raises, and I know we'd all love to have him on the show, but I really don't think it's fair to permit Andy to leave the group for six hours each day so that he can regenerate in his alien sustenance pod. The way I see it, he can go introduce *Survivor* to his own planet (provided he pays the proper licensing fee, of course). Tori Spelling, however, is in. I know, I know, we'd long ago rejected her. But last night her father bought the island we're doing the show on. And no, I have no inside knowledge of how much he had to pay to purchase Australia.

One of the questions that's still left to be hashed out is the matter of the million-dollar jackpot: Should it go directly to the famous person who wins *Celebrity Survivor* or to a charity of his or her choice? On the one hand, I know that a lot of worthy causes are making their cases to the contestants. Martha Stewart's answering service has been besieged by calls from a number of charitable concerns, including Our Lady of the Utensilly Confused, which helps inner-city youth escape poverty by mastering the correct placement of the fish fork.

Bill Clinton is keen to compete for a charity that resonated with him like few others during his presidency – the Foundation for the Heretofore Undiscovered Illegitimate Children of Former U.S. Presidents Born After 1945. And Mr. T has announced that no matter what we decide, his winnings would be earmarked for Flavor Flav House, which for years has been helping black youths cope with a variety of hunchback ailments that stem from years of wearing cumbersome hood ornaments around their necks.

On the other hand, some contend that leaving the charities out of it would result in a much more intriguing and sincere competition. Undeniably, a contestant's mindset would tend to be more ruthless if the financial reward were his or hers to keep. And of course, there's nothing to stop the winner from handing the money to charity anyway. Personally, I'm swayed by this case, and that will be my recommendation to the network: the winner of *Celebrity Survivor* should receive the million dollars, with the Internal Revenue Service taking half that in taxes and, in most cases, the other half in back taxes.

&$*!#!

The Book Club Guide to Talking About *The Osbournes: The Official Biography.*

Discussion points:

1. Begin by comparing *The Osbournes* to other books that were published in largish type, featured an abundance of one-syllable words, and took you less than an hour to read.

2. How is the love a drug-ravaged, hearing-impaired, marble-mouthed father has for his son or daughter different from his love for being left the hell alone to wallow in the silent, tomb-like confines of his damaged mind?

3. What is the symbolic importance of profanity in *The Osbournes*? Does it reflect the family unit's dysfunction and its broad disconnect with the taboos of what we might consider "normal" society? Or does it reflect a desperate need to pad the book by forty-eight pages so that people might be more willing to drop thirty-five dollars for it?

4. Is it true, as some critics contend, that if you read the book backwards, it reveals sinister instructions from the devil

himself? If so, discuss the progress of your personal mission to fulfil Lucifer's sinful directive by wreaking havoc and a profound evil across the land.

5. How have the intricate details of Ozzy Osbourne's personal collection of devil heads affected the manner in which you arrange and showcase your own personal collection of devil heads?

6. Is it really plausible that a man whose greatest claim to notoriety is having chewed the head off a live animal could abruptly be transformed into a mainstream media darling? Discuss your own personal experiences with the repercussions of orally beheading defenceless critters.

7. One entire chapter of the book is comprised of a series of randomly placed vowels, consonants, numbers, and punctuation marks; there are no "words," as such. What does this say about the author? Is he making a bold and profound statement about the inherent meaninglessness of the iconic-celebrity autobiography? Or did he merely pass out on his keyboard? Discuss.

8. How does Ozzy's attitude towards his children change during the course of the book? Does he become a better parent? Is he a good parent at the beginning of the book? Does he even know he has children? Does he know he's a human being who is currently inhabiting the planet Earth?

9. Discuss the themes that are evident within the book. (Note: Although the author makes frequent reference to

his buttocks – mainly within the context of requesting that someone "kiss" his buttocks or suggesting that someone is a "pain" in his buttocks – the buttocks of the author do not, in and of themselves, qualify as a theme.)

10. How in God's name will the literary world ever recover from this?

THE SCHOOL FOR
ASPIRING SUPERMODELS

Curriculum, Day One

7:30 a.m. Breakfast. Students will be presented with a tempting buffet of offerings, including Camel, Marlboro, and Lucky Strike. Orange juice and croissants will also be served, but not to you.

8:00 Official Welcome. A visiting "professor" from Ford Models New York will set the emotional tone for the semester by wishing luck to all students, except those he thinks are "big fat ugly heifers."

8:10 Students will be allotted five minutes to break into tears, turn to the girl in the neighbouring seat, and whimper, "He's talking about me, isn't he? *Isn't he?* He saw me sneak that Altoids!"

8:15 Orientation. All vending machines on campus are located in close proximity to spacious bathroom stalls, which are equipped with luxurious floor padding – just the thing for bony knees! To ensure efficient use of these facilities, please respect the two-heave maximum.

8:30 Multiple-Choice Quiz (60 mins). A test to ascertain students' basic knowledge of the modelling industry. Sample query: "As an aspiring supermodel, I refuse to get out of bed for anything other than (a) $10,000, (b) $25,000, (c) the slimness-enhancing removal of anywhere from two to six ribs.

9:30 Lecture (30 mins). How to Keep a Straight Face While Modelling an Outfit Constructed Entirely from Saran Wrap, Pipe Cleaners, and Dijonnaise.

10:00 Lecture (60 mins). How to Keep a Straight Face While Referring to the Guy Who Designed the Dijonnaise Get-Up as a "Total, Like, Fashion Genius."

11:00 Seminar (90 mins). Walking: Not as Easy as It Looks. If time permits, students will be given the first of eight in-depth lessons on remembering to turn around at the end of the runway.

12:30 p.m. Working Lunch. Students will visit a trendy bistro, where they will be free to order anything on the menu. Students will then be graded on how effectively they rearrange the contents of their plate to give the impression of having consumed something. Bonus points to anyone who clandestinely fashions their gnocchi into an elegant bracelet.

1:00 Guest Speaker: TBA (30 mins). A current supermodel discusses the heroin-chic look: Achievable with makeup, sure, but it's so much easier just to take heroin.

1:30 Seminar (90 mins). Learning How to Talk to the Media About Your Physical Appearance as Though You Actually Had Something to Do With Obtaining It.

3:00 Nutritional Lecture (30 mins). Cigarettes: No matter how hungry you get, do not eat them.

3:30 Seminar (30 mins). Mastering the Vacant Gaze. As essential a component of the supermodel repertoire as being able to stifle a giggle when insisting you eat whatever you want and never exercise.

4:00 Lecture (60 mins). Proper Posture. Guest lecturer Elle MacPherson will reveal that the key is to imagine there is a steel rod fused to your spine. (Note: To assist in this exercise in imagination, each student will have a steel rod fused to her spine.)

5:00 Free Time. Students are encouraged to adopt a bitchy countenance, gaze menacingly at their rivals, and make scornful remarks about their thighs.

6:00 Potluck Dinner. If you think there'll be anything in those pots, you're out of luck.

7:30 Weigh-In. Any student tipping the scales at more than one hundred pounds will be (a) congratulated on not succumbing to the rampant pressure to maintain a malnourished physique, and (b) immediately expelled.

8:15 Informal Group Discussion. Choosing a Rehab Clinic. Guest lecturers: 437 current and former supermodels. We encourage students to offer a stern no! to any and all desperate pleas for smack.

10:00 Lights Out. If you have any trouble falling asleep, we recommend you count the ribs of your roommate.

DEAR MR. TV ANSWER MAN

I'm going insane! I'm trying to remember the name of a show I recall watching briefly a very long time ago while hovering near death in hospital. It starred Erin Moran, Willie Aimes, that chick from Blossom, *and Bob Saget as the crusty yet understanding Sicilian mobster. Please put me out of my misery!*

Glad to assist. You're thinking of *The Only Show on TV Down Here*, which played non-stop in Hell from 1991 to 1994, at which time it was replaced by reruns of *Enos*.

I'm hoping you can help. My girlfriend and I have a bet riding on this. I say that the Jim Belushi who starred in According to Jim *is the brother of the late John Belushi. My girlfriend says the Jim Belushi who starred in* According to Jim *is a nefarious alien scout deployed by a conquering horde of illiterate interstellar flesh-eaters who are currently massing on the outskirts of our solar system in preparation for their vicious cannibalistic assault upon our defenceless yet succulent species. Loser buys the Pringles!*

Your girlfriend is right, of course, just like she's right when she reckons you really ought to wear a shirt 'neath them overalls, Cletus.

I am offended by the negative characterization of Italian-Americans on The Sopranos. *I demand to see a program that depicts the everyday experiences of honest, hard-working Italian-Americans, the principled people who struggle to earn a living, who are faithful to their spouses and to their families, who contribute in a positive way to their communities. Is that too much to ask?*

You're in luck. There's a new drama series on the fall schedule that's just for you. I'm going from memory here, but I think it's called *The Tedious, Doomed Show That Will Make the XFL Look Like a Ratings Titan.*

I recently read that David Hasselhoff is intent on reviving Knight Rider, *which ran for four seasons during the 1980s. Do you have any more information on this?*

Yes, indeed. The start of production will be heralded by promotional advertisements in the trades and the sudden appearance on this planet of a pale horse: the disagreeable chap in the saddle will answer to the name Death, and he'll ride with a sidekick, a sour bugger by the name of Hell. My sources say they'll first kill with sword, then with hunger, then with death and the beasts of the earth, though the script is said to be in rewrite (Hasselhoff is rumoured to want to replace Death and Hell with two chesty flight attendants). The show will premiere in the fall, at the precise moment the sun becomes black as sackcloth of hair and the moon becomes as blood.

I was watching 8 Simple Rules for Dating My Teenage Daughter, *and the lead actor struck me as awfully familiar. Then the weirdest thing happened: as I stared at him, trying to put a name to the face, my head started slowly bobbing up and down. What gives?*

Allow me to quote from the Web site of the Centers for Disease Control: "Thought to have been eradicated by the mid-1980s, this affliction returned in the late 1990s, coinciding with the explosion of specialty television channels and the unexpected end of the career hibernation of John Ritter. Officially classified as *Somersus jigglitis*, it is more commonly referred to as the Three's Company Jiggles – a motor-function impairment that is rooted in the famously loose brassieres worn by the character of Chrissy. There is only one known cure: prolonged exposure to repeats of *The Golden Girls*."

To Whom It May Concern: I find it unfathomable that Matthew Perry was not nominated for an Emmy and Matt LeBlanc was! Matthew Perry is twice the actor of Matt LeBlanc. At least twice! Matthew Perry is a really excellent actor and he deserves some recognition!

Thank you for your note. May I suggest that in future, when making your anonymous case for the hitherto unperceived thespian genius of the star of such epic cinematic achievements as *Three to Tango* and *Serving Sara*, you employ a selection of blank, elegant stationery rather than a note card embossed with "From the Desk of Matthew Perry."

I'm hoping you can help me. I really want to be a contestant for the next instalment of Survivor *on CBS. What do I need to do?*

Thanks to the Internet, the process you need to follow is quite elementary. Simply log on and, using your computer keyboard, type in to the search engine, "Lobotomist." Find one in your area and don't leave his office until this misguided urge fully recedes.

My girlfriend and I have this, like, bet. She says the Cheech Marin who starred with Don Johnson on Nash Bridges *is the same Cheech who used to do all that totally wickedly funny drug comedy with that Chong guy. But I say the Cheech Marin who starred with Don Johnson on* Nash Bridges *is the same Cheech who, uh, used to, like, do all that totally wickedly funny drug comedy with that Chong guy. Can you, like, help?*

I sure, like, can. Just follow this easy two-step procedure: 1. Strap yourself and your girlfriend into your groovy VW van and pilot that hippie monstrosity until you come upon a sign that states, "Warning: Bridge Out." 2. Depress the accelerator, you reefer-addled degenerate. And please be a sport and take with you the dimwitted mouth breather who screens my mail. Correction, *screened* my mail.

Whatever happened to Catherine Bach, the fox who played Daisy on The Dukes of Hazzard?

Alas, her limb rental expired and she was obliged to return her shapely legs to the Screen Actors Guild property room.

Confidential records indicate they're currently being worn by Chi McBride, the principal on *Boston Public*.

I just totally love all those hunky young guys who've been on American Idol. *My friends and I think they make the most awesome music and they're the hottest cutie-patooties on TV! Can you please please please tell us the best way to reach them?*

With a six-pack of Old Milwaukee, a snug-fitting tube top, and an overreliance on monosyllabic utterances, I'd venture. Should your woeful hormonal imbalance persist into the new year, well, bully for you. The fellows will be appearing nightly in downtown Los Angeles, where they will be standing on a street corner hoisting a sign that declares: "Will Drop Trou for Half-Hearted Shrieky Teenage Adoration."

At some point in the past forty years, I think I saw a blondish woman (or was it a man?) appear briefly in a TV show that was about, oh, something or other and featured a bunch of people. Can you tell me the name of the show, the name of the actress, and the name of at least one of the enzymes with a serine that reacts with diisopropylfluorophosphate.

Finally, a sensible query. *Eight Is Enough*. Rosanna Arquette. Chymotrypsin.

Hey, you're quite a snotty little twerp. What do you think is the best thing on television, Mr. Smarty Pants?

The marvellous little button that turns the wretched thing off.

Ten Signs Your Big New Movie Is Going to Bomb at the Box Office

10. Ebert creates a whole new category of rating for it: middle finger up.

9. Immediately after the glitzy premiere, your posse of sycophants ditches you to hang out with Carrot Top.

8. You look at your driver's licence and it says "Jean-Claude Van Damme."

7. Good "buzz" you've been hearing turns out to be box of killer bees sent over by studio.

6. For some baffling reason, audience at test screening had trouble accepting Kathie Lee Gifford as a Jedi knight.

5. People keep asking, "So what are you going to do now that you're out of show business?"

4. The Motion Picture Association of America rated it X – for Xtra Crappy!

3. Keen-eyed critics seem to have noticed that you had the lead actress fired halfway through production and replaced with a sock puppet.

2. The persistent flock of vultures that's been circling overhead.

1. It was released on video last Thursday.

WHAT'S ON TV TONIGHT IN HELL

	8:00	8:30	9:00	9:30	10:00	10:30
Circle 1	**Dog Eat You.** The premiere of Hell's newest reality series.		**Hell's Funniest Practical Jokes.** Satan dons a fake beard and a white robe and rigs a rudimentary bright, soothing light, leading the eternally damned to believe they've arrived at the Pearly Gates.		**Highway to Heaven.** The return of the inferno's top-ranked sitcom.	
Circle 2	**This Hour Has an Eternity.** A seemingly incessant retrospective of the most tedious Canadian current-affairs programming.		**Court TV.** Gene Roddenberry appeals his sentence of everlasting damnation, insisting that, technically speaking, he really had nothing to do with Star Trek: Voyager.		**The Naked and Painfully Ablaze Chef.**	
Circle 3	**Celebrity Pets.** Tonight: Josef Stalin's mutant hellhound; Dee Dee Ramone's hairball.	**Whose Soul Is It Anyway?** More hilarious improvised damnation.	**Martha Stewart Dying.** Useful tips on how to craft elegant parchment from your scorched, peeling flesh.		**Celine Dion Live.** Just the parts of the performance where she pounds her chest or mentions her kid.	
Circle 4	**Biography.** Continuation of a week-long look at Hell's most depraved fornicators. Tonight: Wilt Chamberlain. Tomorrow: Secretariat.		**The Nanny.**	**Dead Air.** A half-hour's interval to permit the Dark Prince to wallow in the anguished wails of the tortured souls who just endured The Nanny.	**The J. Edgar Hoover Show.** Tonight: J. Edgar reminisces about "those bastard Kennedys" with Jack Ruby. Musical guest: Whichever young rapper got gunned down the previous evening.	
Circle 5	**Helletubbies.**	**Let's Make a Deal With the Devil.** Lucifer personally confers everlasting freedom on anyone with a hard-boiled egg in her purse.	**Hell's Classic Bloopers VII.** A hungover Lucifer sentences Benito Mussolini to an "eternity here in Heaven...I mean Hell! *Hell!*"		**The Nature of Fiery Things.** Tonight: Why do the ever-present pools of lava make your ankles all ouchie?	

WHAT'S ON TV TONIGHT IN HELL

	8:00	8:30	9:00	9:30	10:00	10:30
Circle 6	**Approacheth the King.** An inside glimpse at how Hades is preparing for the eventual arrival of Hugh Hefner.		**8 Simple Rules for Rooming with Bob Crane.**	**Beverly Hills 9021ohmigod My Feet Are On Fire!**	**CSI:** Circle 6	
Circle 7	**Trading Spaces.** Adolf Hitler works wonders with Benny Hill's tiny patch of befouled terrain.		**Days of Our Tormented Afterlives.** Britney confesses to a stunned Ridge that she's been surreptitiously harvesting mortal souls with a deformed imp named Rex.		**Behind the Damnation.** A look back at the career of Lucifer and his triumphant struggle to overcome his debilitating addiction to brimstone.	
Circle 8	**Wheel of Perpetual Misfortune.** Two new contestants attempt to defeat returning champion Sid Vicious.		**Celebrity Boxing.** Tonight: Pol Pot vs. Bing Crosby.		**Heaven This Evening.** A nightly, taunting glimpse at the afterlife in The Other Place. Tonight: Walter Matthau gets a soothing back rub from a trio of busty Swedes; a naked Jack Lemmon eats a nine-pounc lobster.	
Circle 9	**Hey, My Face Is Melting!**	**Hey, My Face Is Melting!**	**Hey, My Face Is Melting!**	**Hey, My Face Is Melting!**	**The Best of Hey, My Face Is Melting!**	**Hey, My Face Is Melting!**

FILM REVIEW

Pud!

Good news, film fans: the first genuine blockbuster of summer 2008 has finally arrived, and none too soon for entertainment-hungry moviegoers and a cash-starved industry. Last weekend's box-office take was the smallest in two years, due largely to the unexpectedly tepid reaction to *Waterworld 2: Look, Dude, More Water!*, starring Kevin Costner and Pauly Shore, and the romantic comedy *The Horny Widow*, starring Heather Graham's Naked Breasts, Brendan Fraser, and, in a cameo role, the Rest of Heather Graham. But insiders expect that glum trend to change rather abruptly with today's much-hyped release of *Pud!*, the picture for which thousands of nerds have stood in line for months, forsaking their jobs and their social lives and their personal hygiene and maybe even a thing or two that involved them actually having to forsake something.

Your loyal critic was, you may recall, among those who expressed a certain degree of skepticism when Miramax chief Matt Drudge first announced plans to craft a feature-length, $275-million motion picture from a wordless, two-panel Dubble Bubble comic. But in the wake of the runaway financial success of *Spider-Man* in 2002, and following on the successful release of such big-budget productions as *Daredevil* and *Hulk* and, a year after that, *Frankenberry: The Movie*, studios eventually came to realize there was a dwindling roster of exploitable characters in the lucrative comic/cartoon pantheon.

The ensuing frenzy reached what many believe to be its financial and creative nadir in the fall of 2005, with the green-lighting of the ill-fated *Scrappy-Doo* trilogy (De Niro was magnificent as the snarky, diminutive canine – but those scripts!) and the hurried, conflict-ridden production of *Rush Hour 5*, starring Jackie Chan and the Keebler Elves. The resulting film was such a worldwide financial disaster that Fox executives were inconsolable, even after the movie captured seven Academy Awards.

First optioned in 2004, *Pud!* chronicles one of the amusing moments in the irreverent life of the famously ball-capped, blank-faced boy. In the initial draft of the script, which largely stayed true to the spirit of the original comic, Pud relaxes in a pool atop a flotation device that's shaped like a horse. He passes by a portly man who is standing in the pool, smoking a cigar. The cigar comes into contact with the horse-shaped flotation device and – spoiler alert! – catastrophic hilarity ensues.

Alas, studio executives were unhappy with this screenplay and brought in several teams of script doctors. At one point, Pud was transformed into a freedom fighter in Sierra Leone; at another, he was a boy dressed up as a girl dressed up as a boy, a premise that producers ultimately concluded would make for too great a headache when it came to the swimsuit fitting. There was also, for a brief period, a subplot involving the creation of an apocalyptic race of nuclear-powered rabbits (this plot line may ring a bell: after it was scrapped by *Pud!*'s creators, it was hastily incorporated into the script for Michael Bay's long-awaited adaptation of *War and Peace*).

Finally, after twenty-eight drafts, the studio pronounced itself satisfied with what was, in the words of Mr. Drudge, "*Pud!*'s script as it should be – an organically derived template for a much more powerful, compelling, and entertaining film than originally envisioned." Skeptics were quick to point out that, in the end, the only tangible alteration to the first draft was that the horse-shaped flotation device had been changed to a pony-shaped flotation device. The dissenters had even more reason to ridicule *Pud!* when, months later, the studio abruptly fired Quentin Tarantino, even though the director of *Pulp Fiction* and, more recently, *Mary-Kate and Ashley's Wacky European Adventure* had himself come to the conclusion that his controversial, improvised denouement, which featured the brutal, hyper-stylized beating of the cigar-smoking man, incongruously set to a peppy 1970s pop tune, "might jeopardize the film's G rating."

With a running time of 145 minutes, *Pud!* does eventually come to tax the narrative heft of a wordless, two-inch comic. And surely, there will be some critics who take issue with certain of the film's narrative devices, specifically a seventy-minute scene that, while officially classified by the producers as a "dream sequence," appears in fact to be footage captured accidentally when the cinematographer left his hand-held digital camera running while he and the rest of the crew ate lunch. But there is no denying the film is a visual marvel. It showcases the latest generation of Computer Graphic Imaging, which was first used last winter after Bruce Willis suffered a tragic grimacing mishap. The trauma forced filmmakers to digitize the actor's caddish smirk for several scenes near the conclusion of *Die Hard VI: Would You Just Die Already?*

The Dubble Bubble frontman is fashioned from the same CGI technology, and the results were so true to life that Pud stormed off the set in a snit over the absence of soy-based products on the catering table. His brief, stormy relationship with Winona Ryder brought yet more notoriety to the production, not least when she presented him with the gift of a new cowboy hat. Turned out that Ryder had swiped it off Woody from *Toy Story*.

THE SEASON OF FAWN

Gazing out each year into the ever-expanding mass of truckling, kitten-soft programming related to the Academy Awards, it is possible to come to only one conclusion: You are a lying bastard. And when I say You, I am of course referring to the collective You. The You that keeps bellyaching that the Oscars run too long. The You that sighs heavily during the introduction of yet another ostentatious interpretative dance number featuring scantily clad Disney characters. The You that grouches profanely at Your defenceless television in a futile attempt to get Richard Gere to stop yakking about Tibet. Your lips say You want less Oscar. The middle finger You flip towards the screen when, two hundred minutes into the show, the president of the Academy of Motion Picture Arts and Sciences waddles to the microphone and goes on for roughly an eon about how movies are magical, inspiring, a national treasure, etc. – that finger says You want less Oscar. But Your clicker thumb betrays the fact that You really want more. More pre-awards programming. More post-awards programming. Perhaps even more of that pre-post-awards business where they actually dole out the golden vanity hardware.

For celeb-centric channels such as E! and Star!, and for such star-praising parasitic fanny smooches as *Entertainment Tonight* and *Access Hollywood*, it is all about the Drama. (When a broadcast from E! in the United States is simulcast on Star! in Canada, you just know you're in for a lot of enthusiastic! verbal! punctuation! about celebrities!) And the Academy Awards (Motto: Trying to Live Down the Whole *Driving Miss Daisy* Victory Thing Since 1989!) offers six peerless weeks in which to dramatically speculate upon such suitably urgent inquiries as, How awesome are the nominees? Which of the awesome nominees is likely to be judged the awesomest? And, more pressing yet, how *totally* awesome are the nominees? It's like a fifth season that exists only within the confines of the greater Los Angeles area: after winter and before spring comes the season of fawn.

The Oscar "pre-show," the annual orgy of fashion criticism, insipid chatter, and thoughtful speculation regarding how Melissa Rivers manages to refrain from slapping a roll of duct tape across the cavernous piehole of her lewd, abrasive mother, has in recent years become as much a part of the Academy Awards as counterfeit humility and intrepid cleavage. Millions of people tune in each year to find out who's wearing what and who's wearing whom and, most important of all, who's wearing a dress that's flimsy enough to potentially allow for the spontaneous emergence of anywhere from one to two breasts, an occurrence that would simultaneously delight heterosexual men in 198 countries. Still, as someone who's attended the Oscars, I must reveal that folks at home never get to see the most entertaining aspect of the red-carpet arrivals. Early in the afternoon, a few hours before the Oscar ceremony, Joan Rivers invariably makes a grand entrance of her own and preens to the folks in the bleachers, who by then have been sitting in wait for upwards of six hours and who dutifully applaud, thus revealing the debilitating effects on the brain of prolonged exposure to the sun. Watching the pre-show from home offers unparalleled comfort and the ability to discuss Tom Cruise's sexuality without fear of legal repercussions, but only in person, only in the bleachers, can you witness the quintessential Hollywood sight of determined young publicists conspiring to sneak their A-list clients past Joan Rivers, thus avoiding such profound queries as "Are we the playthings of God?" and, more often, "Whoa, baby, how do you keep those puppies from popping right out?" (Concluding an insipid chat with Chow Yun-Fat one year, Joan turned to the camera, took a deep breath, ditzily shook her six million dollars' worth of borrowed earrings, and opined, "It's wonderful to see so many Asians here." The microphone didn't pick it up, but I'd wager Chow was simultaneously remarking in his native tongue, "How noble the Americans are to give live television programs to their halfwits.")

In 2003, on the occasion of the 75th Academy Awards, a U.S.-led military force was in the initial stages of an attack on the tyrannical Iraqi regime of Saddam Hussein. There was speculation the Oscars would be postponed, just as the

Emmys had been in the aftermath of the terrorist attacks of 9/11. Ultimately, organizers determined that Americans wanted the show to go on. Or rather, they determined that certain Americans wanted the show to go on – namely, those Americans who run ABC and the Academy of Motion Picture Arts and Sciences, who had already sold out four hours' worth of prime-time commercial advertisements at top dollar. At a news conference, the show's producer, Gil Cates, declared that in an effort to be sensitive to the fact that American soldiers were dying in Iraq, he and his collaborators would try to foster a more "appropriate" atmosphere for a wartime awards show. No, he did not mean that, in a gesture of appreciation to the men and women of the American military, the obligatory gift basket given to Oscar presenters in exchange for their gruelling twenty seconds of TelePrompted banter would have a retail value corresponding to the annual salary of a U.S. army private. What Cates meant was that, for the first time in memory, the red carpet outside the Academy Awards would be rolled up, though sadly not while Joan Rivers was standing on it.

Come Oscar night, deprived of their standard perch from which to dish and ditz, Joan and Melissa ended up across the street, broadcasting from a hotel, while their luckless producers descended on the arriving limousines and attempted to coax reluctant A-listers to stroll over for a tedious exchange of platitudes. An hour into the show, Rivers and Rivers had chatted with such marquee names as Shirley Jones and, um, Shirley Jones's husband. Eventually they gave up and debated such urgent global matters as how one successfully negotiates a flight of stairs in a slinky, rump-hugging gown. Slowly, was the conclusion.

"I want to say something right at the start of this whole damn thing!" Joan Rivers hollered as the show began, right about the time that CNN was leading its newscast with a story on the latest American fatalities. "The war is terrible! It stinks! But it's my job to entertain.... God gave me the gift to make you laugh, and I am damn well going to be funny tonight!" And she *was* funny – hilarious, in fact, though not in the way she might have intended. Personally, I wasn't snickering *with* Joan so much as I was snickering at the mental image of punching her in the face. With an array of flippant, condescending remarks about her nation's military personnel, she conclusively proved that the only thing worse than Joan Rivers ignoring the war in Iraq on Oscar night was Joan Rivers acknowledging the war in Iraq on Oscar night. About the only solace a sentient being could muster came from the revelation that the pre-show was being transmitted all the way to Iraq, for viewing by members of the U.S. Armed Forces. So then, technically at least, it was possible that Joan Rivers could ultimately wind up performing her shtick in front of a panel of judges in The Hague.

Prior to the 75th Oscars, conventional wisdom had it that sympathetic starlets might be moved by events in Iraq to reject saucy designer frocks in favour of more conservative garb, a mindset that confirms that many Hollywood actresses ponder global issues only in terms of their potential effect on their chest. War in Iraq? Homeland terror alert at orange? For

Heather Graham, this meant wearing a dress that was only *partially* see-through. Damn you, Saddam Hussein. Damn you and your infernal despotism.

In uneventful times, there is a charming pomposity to the Oscars and its attending sycophancy, to this annual display of American celebrity firepower, media bootlicking, and collagen injections. It's not only a good time; it's a way for Americans to declare to the world that everything is so darn swell in the U.S. of A. that the nation can afford to devote the better part of its free time to fawning over attractive people who earn millions of dollars for making out with J.Lo in front of a bunch of sweaty Teamsters. But the Academy's refusal to postpone the 75th Academy Awards coated the proceedings in a thick patina of smugness, and the celebrities who arrived flashing their peace signs and sporting their peace pins seemed like supporting players in a comedy of errors. Make love, not war. Or at least make me up one of those wicked Oscar gift baskets, dude! In the days leading up to Oscar night, the show's producers said they reserved the right to scrap the ceremony depending on developments on the war front. Can you imagine how the top-level discussion went on the morning of the show? "Hey, a bunch of Marines died over in Iraq today. Is that enough dead Marines to cancel the show or do we need more dead Marines for that?"

When the time came for the stars to arrive, there was one final surprise for television viewers – and for Joan and Melissa Rivers. It involved the lack of a red carpet, which viewers may not have noticed on account of all the red carpet outside the

Kodak Theater. Producer Gil Cates had made his big emotional statement about how sombre times mandate more sombre proceedings, and he had ordered Joan and Melissa and their facelifted ilk to get off Oscar's property. However, there was a red carpet and there were red-carpet interviews – but only on the host network's "official" pre-show. Brilliant! Celebrities were spared the awkwardness of facing questions about the war and stuff, but Cates did it without sacrificing the traditional assembly line of hotties sauntering up the red carpet for ABC's cameras. A few weeks later, the American news media would marvel at the absurd nature of the propaganda being spouted by Iraq's information minister, Mohammed Saeed al-Sahaf, who would gain a peculiar, fleeting fame for denying the very existence of American troops on the outskirts of Baghdad. It's probably a tactic he picked up from watching the Oscars. Red carpet? What are you talking about? *There's no red carpet!*

Granted, that's pretty cynical, but Hollywood has worked hard during the past decade to make us think that way, exposing us regularly to hazardous levels of its reflected glory. Hands up all of you who, during the course of the past several years, have not delighted in deriding the proliferation of televised awards shows, in gruffly ridiculing the shameless abundance of showbiz butt-slappers. Come on, keep up those hands so I can count. One . . . two . . . Okay, you can put both hands down now, Mary Hart.

It used to be the Oscars and the Emmys and the Grammys. That was the sum total of annual, four-hour, prime-time frenzies of self-congratulation, aristocratic indulgence, and chronic bulimia. Nowadays, a conga line of all-American obsequiousness snakes merrily through the television schedule. Like sober guests at a wedding, we watch aghast as chunk after dorky chunk of award hardware is carted off, each kitschy piece destined to spend an eternity in abject servitude to the walloping ego of a film or television celebrity. Even now, Ernest Borgnine must gaze at his Oscar and think to himself, Hey, the public really deserves to see me in more movies!

Like you, I used to marvel at the fact that celebrities would show up for the MTV Movie Awards and the Blockbuster Entertainment Awards, that they'd have Giorgio Armani whip them up a tux for the World Stunt Awards or the TV Land Awards. But then it happened. I was watching the Third Annual TV Guide Awards, just sitting there, listening to an acceptance speech by Bette Midler. And I was struck by a pop-culture epiphany of a magnitude not experienced since it collectively dawned on human civilization that, hey, wait a minute – *Billy Joel actually sucks!* I had seen the light, and the light was Bette Midler, and Bette Midler said unto me: *More awards shows. We need many, many more awards shows.*

To say the least, this view runs contrary to conventional wisdom, not to mention most plausible claims of sanity. But Bette Midler said this unto me in the way she accepted her award for Best Actress in a New Series (for her show *Bette*, which, alas, had already been cancelled by the time the Third Annual TV Guide Awards made it to air). Approaching the podium after grasping her trophy – the winners in all categories were selected by readers of *TV Guide* – Midler quipped, "And to think I'd been using *TV Guide* as a coaster all these years!" She followed that gentle dig with a thoroughly contemptuous summation, in which she thanked all of the periodical's readers who "pulled their stiff little fingers from their remotes and voted for me." How classless! How boorish! *How amusing!*

That's when it hit me: Why do we watch awards show? To be entertained. And what could be more entertaining than the sight of the narcissistic Hollywood hordes all dolled up and kissing the ass of freaking *TV Guide*, the magazine that people take care to hide when company's coming over? What could be more entertaining than the thought of the mega-rich and mega-famous forsaking a jaunt to the Caymans to spend three interminable hours next to a malodorous seat-filler? Midler wasn't the only winner to take a jab at the evening's hosts. Ray Romano, a sitcom star in his very early forties, fondly recollected how he'd been watching the annual program "since I was thirty-nine years old." And Brad Garrett, who plays his brother on *Everybody Loves Raymond*, intoned: "*TV Guide*, I don't know what to say: if it wasn't for you, my kitchen table would [wobble]."

It made for a rare and precious atmosphere during the ceremony: on the one hand, you could tell that few of the winners seemed to hold their award in anything approaching high regard, and fewer still offered anything but snarky barbs for *TV Guide* and its readers. Yet, on the other, almost all of the nominees were there, prompting the obvious question:

How low-rent an awards ceremony would you need to concoct before celebrities finally started to send their regrets? The First Annual Shut-ins of America TV Awards? The Radio Shack Cable-Splicer Salesman of the Year TV Awards? The Golden Globes? Oh, the laughs we will have finding out!

Far and away one of the most inadvertently amusing fawnapaloozas already on the airwaves is the Teen Choice Awards, which in its 2002 instalment deftly made clear that kids just can't catch a break these days. During the ceremony, Sarah Michelle Gellar was named the year's Choice Movie Actress: Comedy, and promptly expressed her gratitude by declaring to her shrieking admirers, "You're the reason we make movies!" Great, just great. Today's teenagers are already struggling with their own physical and emotional changes, not to mention the challenges of peer pressure. And now they're forced to deal with the guilt of having been responsible for *Scooby-Doo*.

The appeal of this particular two-hour beatification, at least to someone whose teen years expired right around the same time as leg warmers and A Flock of Seagulls, rested in its hilarious visual dichotomy: the moist, red faces of horny, squealing teens in the audience juxtaposed with whichever cutaway shots the director could cobble together in which a movie, television, or music star didn't look too weirded out or genuinely fearful of the horny, squealing teens and their moist, red faces. Tobey Maguire was there and, in the brief flashes in which he was featured, the star of *Spider-Man* had the look of a fellow who was spending a nice, quiet evening strapped to an electric chair. His eyes shifted. His facial muscles tensed. It made you wonder what could possibly have been in the cutaway shots of Maguire that weren't used. Perhaps those clips inadvertently showed the Taser wire that was keeping him immobilized until the final credits.

The Teen Choice Awards are run by Fox in conjunction with *Seventeen* magazine, and are easily distinguished from other awards shows in that only here can 'NSync's Lance Bass earn a nomination *for his acting*. (Actually, that's not fair: Lance was not only nominated for, but emerged triumphant from, the 2002 Lucifer's Choice Awards, broadcast live from the Seventh Circle of Hell.) They have established themselves as the showbiz equivalent of Joe Camel – a seemingly innocuous creation that, on closer inspection, has decidedly unsavoury undertones. No, I am not suggesting that, if regarded in a certain light, at a specific angle, the face of Freddie Prinze, Jr., resembles male genitalia. Rather, this is a reference to the covert propagation of addiction. But in this case, it's not nicotine that's being peddled to young 'uns. It's celebrity. Gotta get 'em hooked early or they might develop an interest in books or something. It's all about perpetuating the star-making machinery behind the popular song. And the popular movie. And whatever it is that Carmen Electra does.

The proof was in the shrieking. The shrieking during the 2002 Teen Choice Awards was constant, unending, ear-shattering – even when the camera happened to show that those in the obligatory pit of hard-bodied carousers near the stage looked very much not to be shrieking. Nor shouting.

Nor doing much of anything except standing around or, in one memorable case, sleeping. In the business, this is known as "sweetening" – the practice of embellishing a soundtrack with appreciative noise in an effort to coax viewers into believing an event was far more, well, eventful than it was.

There was also the curious nature of the tribute to Reese Witherspoon, which included a rather long segment devoted to clips from her movie *Sweet Home Alabama*, which differed in one respect from every other flick in Witherspoon's filmography: it had yet to be released. In the business, this is known as "slipping in a trailer in a brazen attempt to slyly manipulate the moviegoing choices of the fickle yet lucrative teen demographic."

And then there was the fine print that flashed by during the closing credits. Therein, the show's organizers revealed that although the ballots cast by readers of *Seventeen* (along with those who visited the magazine's Web site and Fox.com) were used to assemble the list of four nominees in each category, the winners were in fact selected by "a committee of *Seventeen* magazine and Fox." That's strange. While almost every winner expressed thanks to the teens who voted, I didn't hear a single recipient extend his or her gratitude to the group of shadowy figures talking ominously in hushed tones and glaring sinisterly at one another in the star chamber. For all the talk of teen choices, for all the shrieking done by the red, moist, horny squealers in the audience, the big decisions were, in the end, all made by adults. By adults with a stake in selling magazines and promoting TV shows and movies to teens, no less.

In the business, this is known as "the way the business works."

And it is, of course, all about business – specifically, a brand of convergence that predated the AOL Time Warner kind of convergence, and has proved far more successful. It is perhaps best described as the convergence of lips and ass. Celebrities like to be honoured, and networks like to broadcast the ceremonies in which celebrities are honoured, and journalists like to write and talk about the ceremonies in which celebrities are honoured, because people like to watch celebrities being honoured, because it means companies can sell more hairspray and Cadillacs. They know that, no matter the occasion, we'll keep watching until the penultimate celebrity has been voted off Narcissism Island, leaving only Julia Roberts and the skulls of her vanquished rivals.

Drew Carey is one of the few celebrities who has opined grouchily on the subject of awards show. "There is nothing that would make an award meaningful to me," he said in 2002, during a conversation with television critics. "You know, plumbers don't say, 'Hey, you're a good plumber, here's your award.' Nobody else does that. It's only showbiz people and it's only for publicity. It's a chance to push whatever project or to say, 'Hey, I'm famous.' Swear to God, I have two People's Choice Awards, I have a Cable Ace Award, and they're all in a box in my garage. I don't even display them . . . it's like idolatry to me. . . . Like, oh, people are so needy, not only do they need applause and a giant paycheque but they also need a 'thing' to prove to themselves that they are worthy and good. It's like, holy shit, go see a psychiatrist."

Strange, then, that Carey went on that day to admit to feeling rather jazzed upon discovering that he was to be honoured with a star on the Hollywood Walk of Fame. His level of jazzosity declined sharply, however, the more he ascertained the details of the award. "So at first I was really excited. I went, 'Oh, that's something that's pretty cool.' Then I learned about how they do it." Sorry to spoil the utopian notion that one's prospects of sidewalk notoriety are based solely on talent, but the "how" of it all requires that (a) a potential recipient must be "sponsored" by a studio, and (b) that sponsor must fork over in the vicinity of fifty thousand dollars to secure the honour. Carey pondered these facts and concluded with this erudite bit of commentary: "Fuck."

That same brief commentary was doubtless uttered by ABC executives on the morning after the 75th Oscars. The wartime telecast set a new low in Oscars viewership, if not in necklines. Especially startling was that in many areas of the United States, the finale of the reality series *Joe Millionaire*, which had aired a month earlier, had attracted a larger audience. One can imagine the implications: the 76th Annual Academy Awards will take place at a French château where, after much awkward groping and general, all-round sluttery, it will be revealed that Kevin Costner isn't an Oscar winner after all. There won't be a cash prize, but that revelation alone will make everyone in America feel like a million bucks.

One of the by-products of the purported attempt to deprive these wartime Academy Awards of the usual complement of glitz and flagrant self-congratulation was a relatively shorter ceremony: three and a half hours, down from almost four and a half in 2002. To put that in perspective, the 75th Oscars marked the first time in four years that Billy Bob Thornton failed to get married *and* divorced during the show. For the millions who did watch the 2003 Oscars, the ceremony will be remembered largely for its acceptance speeches, many of which included at least an oblique reference to the just-declared war on Iraq. There were, in fact, so many statements advocating peace that Oscar history might well be served by the following handy rating of the Top Celebrity Peaceniks from the 75th Academy Awards. The celebrities are rated on a scale of one drugged-out hippie to five drugged-out hippies, with five drugged-out hippies being, like, totally awesome, dude.

Chris Cooper

Winner, Best Supporting Actor

REMARK: "In light of all the troubles in this world, I wish us all peace."

AUDIENCE REACTION: Enthusiastic applause.

GLOBAL IMPACT: Negligible. U.S. General Tommy Franks declines to order a wholesale retreat or surrender.

RATING: Two drugged-out hippies.

Pedro Almodovar
Winner, Best Original Screenplay
REMARK: Almodovar dedicated his Oscar to "all the people that are raising their voices in favour of peace, respect of human rights, democracy, and international legality."
AUDIENCE REACTION: Enthusiastic applause.
GLOBAL IMPACT: Negligible. The Spanish director's attempts to be classified as an influential opinion leader in North America were once again stymied by his ridiculous hairdo.
RATING: Three drugged-out hippies.

Nicole Kidman
Winner, Best Actress
REMARK: "Why do you come to the Academy Awards when the world is in such turmoil? Because art is important. . . . At the same time, you say, 'There is a lot of problems in the world and since 9/11 there's been a lot of pain with families losing people, and now with a war, families losing people. God bless them.'"
AUDIENCE REACTION: Tepid applause. General confusion regarding what the hell she was talking about. Collective effort not to giggle aloud when she referred to Hollywood movies as "art."
GLOBAL IMPACT: Negligible, save for the fact that her remarks were so convoluted and pointless that they prompted a small percentage of heterosexual men to stop fantasizing about having sex with her.
RATING: One drugged-out hippie.

Adrien Brody

Winner, Best Actor

REMARK: "My experiences in making this film made me very aware of the sadness and dehumanization of people at times of war, the repercussions of war. Whatever you believe in, if it's God or Allah, may He watch over you and let's pray for a peaceful and swift resolution."

AUDIENCE REACTION: Standing ovation.

GLOBAL IMPACT: Negligible, perhaps because the influence of his eloquent remarks was diminished by the fact that commenting on the war rated as Brody's third priority, after thanking his manager and stuffing his tongue into Halle Berry's mouth.

RATING: Four drugged-out hippies.

Michael Moore

Winner, Best Documentary Feature

REMARK: "We live in the time where we have fictitious election results that elect a fictitious president. We live in a time where we have a man sending us to war for fictitious reasons. . . . We are against this war, Mr. Bush. Shame on you, Mr. Bush, shame on you. And any time you got the Pope and the Dixie Chicks against you, your time is up."

AUDIENCE REACTION: Some cheers. Much booing and vigorous hooting.

GLOBAL IMPACT: Upon hearing Moore's tirade, Donald Rumsfeld, the U.S. secretary of defence, cried a single tear and, well, in Whoville they say that Rumsfeld's small heart grew three sizes that day! He phoned the president and got him to call off the war – and he, he himself, the secretary of defence, carved the roast beast!

RATING: Five totally drugged-out hippies. In a VW van.

Susan Sarandon

Presenter

ACTION: Stops, bows, makes peace sign.

AUDIENCE REACTION: Confusion over whether Sarandon is advocating peace or acting in role of celebrity pitchwoman for Verizon Wireless.

GLOBAL IMPACT: General consensus among middle-aged men that, while Sarandon's relentless activism and general know-it-allity is annoying, they'd probably still do her.

RATING: One soccer mom reminiscing about having been a drugged-out hippie.

SIMPLE WAYS TO MAKE THE OSCARS LESS TEDIOUS

✔ Subject all losers to stern corporal punishment.

✔ At the top of every hour, have security officials appear on stage to conduct a thorough frisking of Halle Berry.

✔ Announce that due to a production snafu, there is only one Oscar statue for the two female acting categories, and if the Best Actress and Best Supporting Actress want it, they damn well better climb into that mud-filled swimming pool and start rasslin'.

✔ All musical numbers to be performed by nerdy duo from PricewaterhouseCoopers.

✔ Traditional dull retrospective replaced with more promising Thirty-Five Years of Gratuitous Nudity.

✔ On way to stage, all winners to be accosted by squeegee kids and change-mooching vagrants.

✔ Obligatory sombre montage of deceased film icons accompanied by audio track of what people *really* thought of them.

✔ Old way of coaxing winners off stage: Orchestra begins playing softly. New way: Warning shot fired over head by FBI sharpshooter.

OSCAR BINGO

B	I	N	G	O
Obligatory reference to show's interminable duration	Audience claps louder for certain dead people	Academy apologizes for whole "giving Costner an Oscar" thing	Winner pauses to acknowledge, French kiss sibling	Comically insincere reference to sanctity of artistic process
Winner mentions agent, accountant, taxidermist, but not spouse	Beefy enforcer "coaxes" Best Actress winner to fork over statue to J.Lo	Heartless, profit-minded moguls unconvincingly depicted as dedicated to quality cinema	Unconvincing stab at appearing humble	Presenter cringes at hokiness of scripted banter
Ill-advised choreography involving absurdly sequinned women	Trouble reading TelePrompTer		Juvenile comic antics involving theatrical opening of envelope	Inside joke about Russell Crowe's libido
Standing ovation feels forced and insincere	Actress wears Armani's new Wanton Trollop line	Accounting firm nerds kinda nervous and sweaty	Black actor wins; director cuts to shots of black people in audience	"You like me, you really like me. Or, possibly, you just despise my rivals."
Seated ovation feels forced and insincere	Half-decent movie revered as epic masterpiece	Obligatory reference to obligatory references to show's interminable duration	"I wouldn't be up here if not for my agent/my lawyer/my pharmacist."	Jack Nicholson suavely impregnates comely seat-filler

How to Write
an Oscar Speech

Excerpts from a pamphlet distributed to Academy Award nominees:

1. The Opening

The exclamations "Wow!" and "Woo-hoo!" and "Oh my God!" are each considered an acceptable way to begin an address upon being presented with an Academy Award. On the other hand, the Academy continues to advise against the use of either "It's about goddamned time!" or "Motherfucker!"

2. The Declaration of Disbelief

Do not, under any circumstances, say, "I'm speechless!" Similarly, do not say anything to the effect of "Golly gee, I didn't even prepare a speech!" Remember, you are a Hollywood movie star. You have an ego so large that it recently began generating its own gravitational field. Everyone knows that for the past six weeks you have thought only about (a) your speech, (b) reminding yourself to vomit after each meal so you don't look fat when you deliver your speech, and (c) ways to pretend you didn't prepare a speech.

3. The Insincere Expression of Inferiority

We cannot be firm enough in recommending against the utterance of the familiar phrase, "I don't deserve this." First of all, no one will believe that you, a major Hollywood movie star, genuinely harbour this sentiment. Second, everyone who saw your movie will already know this to be true.

4. The Obligatory Reference to Fellow Nominees

The four losers (or, as we in the Academy prefer to identify them, the four individuals to whom the Oscar did not go) have just seen vanish what may be their only chance to win the industry's most prestigious award. The last thing they want is you mentioning them by name, thus prompting television cameras to swoop in to record their awkward attempts to appear "calm" and "together" and "happy for you" when in fact all they really want is for you to be inexplicably devoured by a prehistoric, reptilian predator.

5. The Display of Emotion

Crying is acceptable, but the Academy urges you to keep a handle on it. You just won an award; you did not just witness the birth of your child, survive a life-threatening operation, or purchase a pair of Prada pumps at half-price. Recommendation: Moist eyes, deep breathing, a shake of the head to indicate a healthy sense of disbelief. Keep in mind that Mira Sorvino was awarded one of these things, and what the hell ever happened to her?

6. The Reference to Political Causes or Beliefs

This is frowned upon by the Academy, and highly inadvisable. We say this not in an effort to curtail or otherwise infringe upon your constitutional right to free speech. Rather, our concern is more practical. We have all worked very hard as an industry to ensure that the North American public spends more time thinking about movie stars than, say, global affairs or community initiatives or their families. Bottom line: People have only so much free time. If you want them to worry about Tibet, fine, but don't come crying to us if your next picture bombs because Americans were too busy heeding your call to pressure Japan or Korea or Canada or whoever into letting the Tibetinards do whatever it is they can't currently do.

7. The Thank-Yous

Note to winners: You are in the entertainment business. Is it asking too much for you to refrain from giving a speech that has all the vigour and creative élan of an airport boarding call? Reading off a long list of names known only to industry types is inexcusably boring; a simple thanks to everyone ("You know who you are") sounds insincere. Best solution: Cite no more than three people, and explain why they deserve thanks. Announce that a complete list of thanks will be posted to your official Web site. Then, to ensure everyone visits your Web site, announce that the thank-you list will be posted alongside some candid photographs of your naughty bits.

8. The Exceeding of the Time Limit

No great offence, frankly, assuming you're prepared to direct a clever remark at the orchestra leader, such as "I ain't leavin'!" or "You can play, but I'm gonna keep talkin'!" or "I can afford to have you and your family killed a thousand times over, baton boy!"

9. The Farewell Gesture

Hoisting the Oscar skyward while saying "Thank you so much" or "I'll remember this forever" is standard protocol. However, shouting "I'm the king of the world!" – even if it is a line from your movie – is considered bad form, as is thrusting your Oscar in the direction of your rivals and braying, "Nyah, nyah, nyah-nyah nyah!"

10. Miscellany

If, upon hearing your name announced, you feel you must neck with a relative, all we ask is that you at least consider selecting a relative of the opposite sex.

THE APOLOGY:
A ONE-ACT PLAY

Dramatis Persona: The Celebrity

Setting: A news conference in a hotel ballroom. Microphones are positioned on an otherwise bare table. Television reporters adjust their hairpieces.

The Celebrity sits down. Flashbulbs! A CNN correspondent is heard saying, "He's finally here, so let's listen in live . . ."

THE CELEBRITY: Okay. First, I want to thank you for coming all the way out here today. I know it's a Saturday, and you all have better things to do with your lives. Especially all you film critics, who are probably supposed to be at film-critic school right now, learning more synonyms for "crap." [*pauses for laughter*] Maybe you shouldn't waste so many of them describing *my* pictures! [*pauses for fits of hysteria among gathered press*]

But seriously. I was looking out at you all just now and it occurred to me that I recognize many of your faces from my last news conference of this unfortunate nature. [*unintelligible voice from offstage*] Huh, what's that, Frankie? [*unintelligible voice*] Oh, right, the last one was actually in Maui, after that bit of unpleasantness with Don Ho. [*unintelligible voice from offstage*] Eh, what's that, Frankie? [*unintelligible voice*] Right, that's right. All I said was, "Interesting name. I assume that means your wife is a Ho, too." [*much laughter*] And the guy comes at me, guitar swinging, tries to strangle me with his lei. Decking him was self-defence, plain and simple – although, as I said to the press in Maui, and before that to the constables who detained me, I was wrong to have escalated the confrontation in the manner I did. Which is why I imme-diately offered to pay half the cost of the laser surgery required to cover up those teeth marks. [*pause*] Ho. Come on, that's a funny name! You know, over the years, I think I may have spent some time with several of his daughters. Candy the Ho. Trixie the Ho. Don raised some real pros, if you know what I mean, heh-heh. [*pause*] And if you don't, I'll just have to come out and tell you I'm talking about hookers! [*gales of laughter*]

Anyway, what I meant was the news conference before that, the one when I was sitting here, in this very hotel ballroom, wearing the sling and the patch over one eye. And the handcuffs. Speaking of which, can I just take a moment here at the outset to say that the Four Seasons has just this week rescinded the lifetime ban it had imposed on me, which is excellent news and much appreciated, and that all medical evidence points to both the bellboy and the valet being put back on solids as early as the summer? Isn't that great? That'll make life in those wheelchairs worth living, fellas!

I'm sorry to say the news is not so good for the concierge. I myself am not a doctor – although you might remember that

I played one in my 1998 film *I'm OK, You're the Problem, Bitch!*
And may I just say that I still can't believe the studio botched
the marketing of that one. Shalit, you know what I'm talking
about, right? Damn right you do. I mean, I worked my ass off.
Twelve, sometimes fourteen hours a week. I pitched in to
rescue what I have to say was a very iffy script. And the result
was a deep, thoughtful meditation on the fragile nature of the
social contract that binds us together as human beings. But
those studio hotshots, man, I tell ya. Those suits spot two or
three homicidal rampages in a picture – they get so much as a
glimpse of a genetically engineered, man-eating super-puma
or a bloody hostage standoff at the Playboy Mansion – and
immediately their feeble, pre-programmed minds start
thinking, "Action movie." It still burns me, man. I'm telling
you, our Oscar credibility was shot from the moment they cut
that first trailer – the one that played up the alien mind-
control ray that forces the Playmates to simultaneously
disrobe and indulge in the Sacred Sponge-Bath Ritual before
they invade St. Bart's for that climactic pillow fight.

Anyway, like I say, I'm not a doctor, but the bugaboo with
the concierge apparently has something to do with the precise
angle at which the ballpoint pen entered his aortic valve. They
tried to explain it to me, but hospital dramas are just so tired.
I'm like, "Everything here's an *itis* or an *ism*. I'm not George
Freaking Clooney! *No hablos, señor!*" Anyhoo, long story
short, I visited the concierge the other day. Went to make my
peace. I apologized. He's still in the coma, but I'm pretty sure
he heard me. He twitched a couple of times anyway, which I

took as a sign of forgiveness. I admitted I was in the wrong, that nothing could have justified the way I treated him. [*pause*] Although, at the same time, when a frequent guest of your hotel calls down and asks for some ice, you really ought to just hop to it and get him the ice. Am I wrong about that? You don't say, "Yes, sir, right after I help the paramedics tend to the prime minister of France."

But enough reminiscing. On to the business at hand. Okay, where should I start? [*unintelligible voice from offstage*] What's that, Frankie? [*unintelligible voice*] Right, Ebert's Lexus. Right. Well, as most of you know by now, Roger had some rather unfriendly things to say about my newest movie, *Smells Like Love*. A few hours after his review came out, I happened to bump into him as he was coming out of the shower in the ensuite bathroom of his house. Some words were exchanged, and then I left, and I guess on my way out maybe I flicked my cigarette and it must have got into his car through the window or something. I don't know. All I do know is that, soon enough, *boom*, there are flames twenty feet high, and Ebert's coming at me across his front lawn, the towel around his waist loosening with every step. [*pause*] And let me just say this about what I saw: Thumbs down! [*gales of laughter*] Not that I'm a fag or anything. I'm just saying.

Now listen, I know the cops have been trying to impress you with big words like "accelerant" and "conclusive evidence." And I know a certain amount of attention has been paid, especially by those in the district attorney's office, to some of the words I may or may not have directed at Roger, whom I consider to be a dear friend, and with whom I very much hope to work in the near future. [*forms baby finger and thumb into telephone, puts to ear, and whispers: "Call me, Roger!"*] The specific area of focus seems to be my alleged utterance of the sentence [*consults paper*]: "As God is my witness, I am going to hunt you down, make you my bitch, and then strangle the life out of your big fat fuck of a body, you big fat fuck!"

Oh, I probably shouldn't have repeated that on live television. Sorry, CNN. Aw, hell, maybe it'll get you some ratings. Fuck. Fuuuuuuck. Fucky fuck fuckity fuck fuck! The numbers are soaring as we speak. Friends calling friends, telling them to tune in, that guy who won the Oscar for *Fatal Fatality* is cussing up a storm! [*unintelligible voice from offstage*] Huh, what's that, Frankie? [*unintelligible voice*] Right. Ozzy got paid millions to do that on TV, and I'm giving it away for free! Fuck. [*hilarity ensues*] But the point is this: maybe I said those things to Roger, and maybe I didn't. But if I did say those things to Roger, I can assure you that I was speaking metaphorically. That's the language of show business, you know: metaphors. And so when I said I was going to make Roger Ebert my bitch and then kill him, if in fact I said that, then what I was really saying was "Roger, you are I are experiencing a difference of opinion, and I look forward to a respectful debate on the issue." Except I said it metaphorically, assuming I said it at all. All I can add to this is that in future I will endeavour not to drink so much on occasions in which I find myself angry or unsettled. Drinking does strange things to the coke, man. Strange things.

I want to thank my wife for standing beside me through this dark time. She's not actually here today, so she's not standing beside me in person, but I know she's standing beside me at her mother's house, where she went a couple of nights ago with the children. Call me, honey. Don't make me freeze the bank accounts this time. My publicist, my personal assistants. My parole officer, my bail bondsman. They've all been with me a long time now. My manager, my agent, my lawyer, they've stood behind me, too, and I really appreciate that. [*unintelligible voice from offstage*] Huh? What's that, Frankie? [*unintelligible voice*] Right. Right, I was being a little insensitive there. Seems to be a common problem of mine. The truth is that "stood behind me" was, as many of you know, a poor choice of words as it pertains to my agent. Dex hasn't officially [*makes air quotes*] "stood" since that unfortunate night on my yacht, when he [*makes air quotes*] "tripped and fell" and busted his nose or his spine or whatever. I probably shouldn't have made that second set of air quotes, now that I think about it. Anyhoo, Dex is too much the gentleman to ever say anything himself, but the consensus among those present seems to be that I played at least a supporting role in his misfortune. Understand that I have only a foggy memory of events, owing to an uncharacteristic overindulgence in libations [*knowing laughter*], but the conventional wisdom has it that I not only tackled Dex after he disputed the thread count of my Egyptian cotton sheets, but stomped him repeatedly upon the neck. [*unintelligible voice from offstage*] Huh?

What's that, Frankie? [*unintelligible voice*] Right, I also may have hindered first-aid efforts by yelling, "Let the fucker bleed!" Not that many people probably heard me over the sound of my automatic weapon.

Anyway, the important thing is that Dex is such a good sport, he hardly ever complains about his lot in life – although maybe that's the morphine drip talking, huh, Dex? Look at the pathetic bastard smiling. He has no idea what I'm talking about. [*laughter*] He's a hero to me. A role model. Plus, all the suits in town feel so guilty looking down at Dex that they always sweeten their offers just to get the paralyzed bastard out of their office! Right, Dex? It's a fucking scream, man! How did you think I got twenty-five million dollars to star in *The Patriotic Veterinarian*? That said, I've got to tell you, I know Dex doesn't exactly have it easy, but at least his hearing was damaged by all that severe trauma to the head. At least he doesn't have to listen to that sound he makes when he uses that straw thing to steer his wheelchair. [*makes exaggerated slurping sound*] God, it's getting on my nerves. But don't worry, Dex, I'd never drop you, man. Our relationship is forever . . . you fucking cripple. [*laughter*]

Now, on to these bogus allegations that have been maliciously asserted by Ms. Angelina Jolie. *Webster's* defines "stalking" as "to follow or observe a person persistently, especially out of obsession or derangement . . ."

(*Fade to black*)

A Selection of Movie Artifacts
and Memorabilia Rejected
by Planet Hollywood

1. Exhibit 65712/33

*A pie chart taken from a financial update prepared by an
accountant to a major A-list Hollywood actor, circa 2000*

The $20-Million Dollar Paycheque
Where Does it Go?

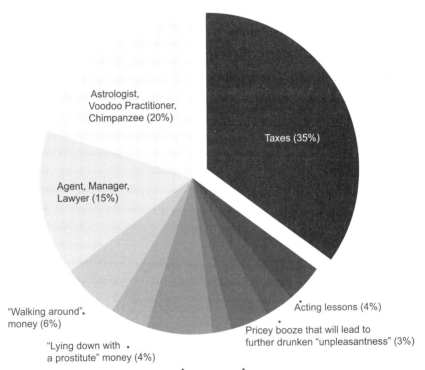

Astrologist,
Voodoo Practitioner,
Chimpanzee (20%)

Taxes (35%)

Agent, Manager,
Lawyer (15%)

"Walking around".
money (6%)

Acting lessons (4%)

Pricey booze that will lead to
further drunken "unpleasantness" (3%)

"Lying down with
a prostitute" money (4%)

Posse upkeep (7%)   Cash settlement
re: drunken "unpleasantness" (4%)

Betty Ford alumni fund (2%)

2. Exhibit 87190/30

Documentation of the first successful translation of the contents of a Hollywood-movie press kit

For decades, these cheerful texts – published in a language known as *propagandese* – had stumped scholars, baffled linguists, and sedated film critics. But decades of painstaking research have finally resulted in a breakthrough: full translation. According to this sunny, happy language, every film is a masterpiece, every movie set a joy on which to work, every cast member a colossal talent. Only with the release in 1999 of an otherwise forgettable feature, *Three to Tango*, was the code cracked and the contents of a press kit translated to common English. The romantic comedy chronicled the story of a struggling Chicago architect (Matthew Perry) who, wrongly thought to be gay by an adulterous client (Dylan McDermott), finds himself obliged to spend time with the client's mistress (Neve Campbell) to ensure she remains faithful.

According to the press kit, *Three to Tango* is "an exciting and very entertaining story," a "helluva movie" that has a "totally unique and original twist" and is performed by "an amazing and very talented actor" (Perry), another "amazing actor" (Oliver Platt), "a truly funny lady" (Campbell), and an "absolutely hysterical" guy (McDermott).

Translation: It's a meek, formulaic stab at romantic comedy featuring a trio of mildly competent actors whose real jobs are in television.

Other excerpted translations:

Propagandese: "It's hilarious and yet has a lot of layers – social commentary and physical comedy along with some very heartfelt moments between characters who are learning how to fall in love." – Freshman director Damon Santostefano

Translation: "Yay, they let me make a movie!!"

Propagandese: "Damon's work is original and cinematic." – Producer Jeffrey Silver

Translation: "Damon routinely washed my car while the lighting guys were setting up."

Propagandese: "It's hard to put in words just how funny Dylan is." – Director Santostefano

Translation: "Dylan is not very funny."

Propagandese: "No other actor has Matthew's ability to be ironic and completely vulnerable at the same time." – Director Santostefano

Translation: "No other actor in his salary range has Matthew's ability to deliver on the big screen the exact same verbal tics and physical gestures that he delivers each week on the small screen."

Propagandese: "Learning something new, challenging myself, getting to know some terrific people and laughing a lot – that is what was most wonderful about *Three to Tango*." – Neve Campbell

Translation: "I did this movie because I needed money to buy stuff."

Propagandese: "In the context of this movie, the worst thing that can happen, does: Oscar [Perry's character] finally falls in love but cannot openly express that love because it would jeopardize everything he's built." – Producer Bobby Newmyer

Translation: "In the context of this movie, the worst thing that can happen, does: we actually filmed and released this movie."

This remarkable breakthrough has made life easier for a whole generation of film critics. Consider these useful translations from the press kit for the Jennifer Lopez movie *Maid in Manhattan*, in which she plays a hotel maid who falls for a wealthy politician.

Propagandese: "We loved that his films (*Smoke, Chan Is Missing*) were antithetical to the genre." – Producer Deborah Schindler, speaking of director Wayne Wang

Translation: "He worked cheap."

Propagandese: "He heard our ideas and scripted a beautiful story." – Producer Elaine Goldsmith-Thomas, speaking of screenwriter Kevin Wade

Translation: "He rented *Working Girl* and *Cinderella* and then did some typing."

Propagandese: "Through Jennifer, we were able to discover the nuances that would make this character real." – Producer Goldsmith-Thomas

Translation: "I tried to tell her that a woman who works as a hotel maid would probably not wake up in a pair of $3,400 Dolce and Gabbana pyjamas, but I couldn't get past her posse."

Propagandese: "Ralph was affable, sweet, and open to exploring his gentler side." – Producer Goldsmith-Thomas on the film's male lead, Ralph Fiennes

Translation: "He fainted when we told him his trailer was going to be one-eighth the size of J.Lo's."

Propagandese: "She has great magnetism and an iconic quality." – Fiennes on J.Lo

Translation: "When the cameras weren't rolling, she never, ever talked to me."

Propagandese: "I tried to give [Ralph] the context he needed to work organically, so that the comedy came out of that character's particular situation. With Jennifer it was more a matter of letting her go, letting her explore." – Director Wang

Translation: "The bitch didn't listen to a damn word I said."

3. Exhibit 12986/09

Discovered in April 1987 in the wastepaper basket of a junior suite at the Four Seasons Hotel Los Angeles, this is widely believed by anthropologists to be an attempt by a critic attending a film junket to craft an upbeat blurb for use in promotional advertisements touting the release of Ishtar, which went on to become a legendary critical and financial flop.

Four Seasons
Los Angeles

Re: Ishtar

Uproarous! ~~Uproarous!~~
~~Hilarious!~~
~~A roller-coaster thrill ride!~~
~~A laugh-out-loud comedy!~~
~~A laugh-out-loud roller-coaster thrill~~
~~ride! (Didn't I use this one on *Terms of*~~
~~*Endearment*?)~~
~~The best movie I've seen this year!~~
~~The best movie I've seen any year!~~
  ~~(Too much)~~
The best movie I saw between 2pm
  and 4pm this past Wednesday!
Magnificent! Amazing! ~~Complete~~
~~and utter horseshit! (Accurate, yes,~~
~~but...)~~
~~Quite possibly the biggest piece of crap!~~
Craptacular! (OK, come on now, focus)

~~Warren Beatty is phenomenal!~~
~~Warren Beatty is hilarious!~~
~~Warren Beatty called me "the fat guy~~
~~with the lisp" during our roundtable~~
~~session!~~

~~A grade-A shit sandwich!~~
~~You won't find a funnier movie this~~
~~summer! (Because you'll be in a~~
~~coma from this one!)~~
I hate my life and I want to die!

218

4. Exhibit 13452/65

Transcript from the first Internet chat room devoted to discussion of the film Crossroads, which represented the feature-film acting debut of pop singer Britney Spears.

Welcome to the Britney Spears chat room! Britney Spears the actress, that is! This room is for discussion about Brit's awesome movie, *Crossroads*! Well, actually, it's just *Crossroads*, without the exclamation mark, although it totally should have had one because it is so awesome! I bet it is anyway! Remember: Respect others and do not disrespect Britney!

NOTYETAWOMAN: omigod! I like totally saw it last night and it was awesome!!!

NOT_A_GIRL: how awesome?!

NOTYETAWOMAN: AWESOME!!!!

OOPS!: that's awesome that it's awesome!!!

NOT_A_GIRL: i heard some big loser guy somewhere saying it's basically just one big long Brit video because mostly all she does is sing.

NOTYETAWOMAN: no way!!! she sang at the beginning and then she sang this other song and that led to this part where she sings and that singing leads to this other song that makes everyone think hey!! this girl should be singing!!! and then she sings a song at the end, except it's not really the end because there's another song!!! But that's totally it. Except for the part where she sings that 'NSync song, but that's so cute they just had to put it in!!!

NOT_A_GIRL: Obviously!

SLAVE_4U: i hear she like totally has an accent!

NOTYETAWOMAN: ya but she only uses it part of the time. probably so her fans know it's all pretend and her voice hasn't really changed! :-)

SLAVE_4U: she's always thinking of the fanz!!

WALTER: Good day! Just out of idle curiosity, and not because I am a creepy pervert controlled by a vivid array of peculiar fetishist urges involving Britney Spears, could you please inform me whether Britney does, at any stage of the movie, remove her clothing?

NOTYETAWOMAN: totally walter!!! first she's in her underwear and then she's in an even smaller pair of underwear and then she almost has sex and then she's in a towel after a shower and then she does have sex! why do you ask?!

WALTER: Sdfsfgdf zzxxt

NOT_A_GIRL: hey walter!! if you want to chat in this room, you're going to have to type faster than that. it's like you're using one hand or something!!! :-)

SLAVE_4U: Boyz!!!

NOTYETAWOMAN: so anyway the worst thing about the movie – and don't worry it's not actually something bad about the movie!!! which is awesome by the way!!! – is that we were sitting behind this, like, totally old guy ;-) and he had a pen and everything and kept writing stuff down and sighing really loudly and totally being a dork.

OOPS!: was he some sort of total freak or something?!

NOTYETAWOMAN: i wish!! he was a movie critic.

NOT_A_GIRL: ewwww!!!! :-(

NOTYETAWOMAN: so anyway i talked to him and i told him to write that the movie is awesome (which it totally is!!) and he said brit's acting style is entirely predekayted (is that even a word???) on cocking her head to one side and blinking very slowly. and i said that is totally not true. she also giggles when she's happy and wears lip gloss when she's totally serious!

NOT_A_GIRL: Lip gloss!! whoa, i wouldn't want to cross her path! Pow!

NOTYETAWOMAN: i told him it was an awesome movie with awesome things to say about things like life. but he just like totally laughed. and then i said i thought it was totally original and brilliant, and he laughed even harder and called it kleecheyed and blah-zay (sp??).

NOT_A_GIRL: French people don't get Brit!!! they'd rather sit around and be depressed and speak French!

NOTYETAWOMAN: and then i said britney is like a way better actress than madonna. and he started to laugh again but then he stopped and he said actually you're right about that one :-)

OOPS!: how many stars is he going to give the movie?

NOTYETAWOMAN: you know i didn't even ask him. but he seemed really really totally happy when the movie ended, so it must be tons!!!

The Fifteen Things I'd Immediately Do If I Ran American Television

1. Personally deliver a herd of feral, rabid reindeer to the home of any subordinate who suggested airing even a single Christmas-related program prior to December 1.

2. Take the trend in reality programming to its logical conclusion by assigning a camera crew to produce a round-the-clock chronicle of the activities of Pamela Anderson's left breast.

3. Reveal my ingenious plan to ensure that *Friends* will never, ever cease production: coax Hollywood's film studios to pay the cast's obscene salaries by uttering the chilling words, "If the show dies, Matt LeBlanc and Matthew Perry are going to have a lot more time to make movies."

4. Decree that every series on television must have a theme song. And then, days later, decree that every series on television must have the theme song from *The Dukes of Hazzard*.

5. Monitor all programming for the next instance in which a character says something along the lines of, "I won't do it. I won't perform in that talent show. There is nothing you could do to make me perform in that talent show," and then, after a quick cut, is revealed to be performing in the talent show. Find the writer of this segment and make him

the guest of honour on my new reality series, *Who Wants to Throw a Bunch of Darts at Some Overpaid Hack?*

6. Install a trap door in front of my desk, strictly for use during visits from surly creditors, hired goons, and people pitching shows starring John Stamos.

7. Immediately green-light *Annoying Celebrity Survivor*, wherein a selection of the medium's most irritating per- sonalities – Connie Chung, Jim Belushi, the People Who First Put Connie Chung and Jim Belushi on Television – would be taken to a remote island, abandoned, and . . . well, that's pretty much it, actually. We'd probably send a camera crew back in a few years for the retrieval of the gnawed skeletal remains and Jim Belushi.

8. Revive the *Battle of the Network Stars* for the sole and selfish purpose of repeatedly watching slo-mo replays of Tiffani Thiessen emerging from the dunk tank.

9. Replace all commercial breaks during episodes of *Cops* with a public-service announcement advising viewers to report to their local hospital for forced sterilization.

10. Coerce Dick Clark to admit tearfully, on live television, that the real reason he always hosts the New Year's Eve show on ABC is "because I have no friends."

11. Do what should have been done long ago: Give Jerry Orbach's hairdo its own spinoff series.

12. At my fickle, tyrannical whim, order actors to swap roles with their peers on another series. For instance, John Ritter would be obliged to switch with Martin Sheen,

thus allowing *The West Wing*'s writers to explore virgin dramatic territory, wherein the President of the United States nukes a rogue Asian nation because of something his pal Larry misheard the previous evening at the Regal Beagle. Meantime, on *8 Simple Rules for Dating My Teenage Daughter*, the girls wonder why Daddy keeps speaking in Latin.

13. Request that Dan Rather try a new signature sign-off, which would require him to look down briefly before assuring America, "Yep, I remembered the pants."

14. Call up Aaron Spelling and declare into the phone, "I have five words for you, good sir – *Love Boat: The Next Generation.*"

15. Lather. Rinse. Repeat. And then, befitting my god-like stature at the pinnacle of America's pre-eminent entertainment medium, repeat *again*.

A Personal Message to
Powerful Hollywood Executives

I admit it: at first glance, this book does not establish itself as the sort of work that should be optioned by a Hollywood film studio. I won't pretend otherwise. There are no intriguing plot developments in this book – nor even, for that matter, a plot, although savvy veterans of the multiplex will realize this shortcoming does not in itself preclude a big-screen adaptation. No one comes of age in this book, nor are there any computer-generated special effects, nor even a single montage that depicts two profoundly different characters falling in love against all odds to the sounds of a bouncy, familiar 1960s pop number. Most damning of all, the book fails to document the determined crusade of a plucky, disadvantaged young woman to triumph over adversity, learn a valuable life lesson, and, along the way, enthusiastically embrace even the slightest pretext for removing her underpants.

But here is the peculiar thing about the optioning of books: most books that get optioned are *never actually made into movies*. Instead, they wind up mired in what's called Development, a boundless swath of creative quicksand in which countless well-meaning writers and producers have misplaced years of their professional lives, not to mention their eight-hundred-dollar shoes. During the Development process, many meetings are convened. Casting is pondered. A budget is debated. A screenplay is commissioned. At which point a powerful Hollywood executive decrees that everything that has so far been pondered, debated, and commissioned shares the unenviable quality of (as it's typically put in arcane industry parlance) "sucking big time." This conclusion invariably leads to many more meetings being convened. Casting is repondered. A budget is redebated. A screenplay is recommissioned. And so on. Not infrequently, the only tangible development that results from Development is the decision to pursue Further Development.

All of these phases – Development, Further Development, Cripes, Are We Still in Development?, The Stage of Yet Further Development That Ensues After the Author, Frustrated by the Endlessness of the Development Process, Commits Suicide – they all cost money. It costs money to consider casting a major motion picture. It costs money to commission a screenplay. It even costs money to debate how much money everything might cost. Which is why it makes sense at this juncture to pause and reflect upon a saying that you folks in Hollywood have about money. Actually, there are at least two sayings that you folks in Hollywood have about money, one of which is "Gimme." But the saying that applies in this case is the other one, a saying that is a variation on the popular morsel of homespun wisdom that contends a penny saved is a penny earned. "In Hollywood," the saying goes, "a fifty-dollar bill saved is an ostentatious way to light your cigar." Wise advice, my friend. Wise advice.

With my book, you know from the get-go that there is absolutely no hope of turning it into a movie. On one hand this is a drag, because here you've gone and optioned a book and now nothing can come of it. But look at it from an alternative perspective: think of the money you'll save! I mean, sure, you're going to have to cut me a cheque for hundreds of thousands of dollars. That is the reality of the situation, and there is no getting around it. *But you'd have to do that no matter which book you'd optioned.* By optioning this book, my book, a book which cannot in any conceivable way be transformed into a major motion picture, you completely eliminate the need to convene meetings. That's at least a couple hundred bucks – money that would have gone into the till at the muffin shop – back in the studio's coffers! Go ahead and offer Nick Nolte a complimentary haircut. *You can afford it!* Better still, neither you nor any of your underlings need to ponder casting, or debate a budget, or commission a screenplay (although, should the urge to commission a screenplay prove irresistible, I'd be willing to take a pass at a first draft in return for six more figures, preferably eights or nines).

Think of it like this: there are two ways that you, a Hollywood executive, can come to be revered as a hero, an indispensable superstar, by your studio:

1. You could be the person to discover and negotiate the film rights to the one book out there that is going to earn the most money of any literary adaptation and maybe grab a couple of Oscars to boot. No denying it, that sounds pretty sweet. Problem is, there are an awful lot of books out there, and not

only would you have to locate and identify this one mysterious, magical, super-special book, you'd probably have to read parts of it, too, just so you don't look like an idiot in the meetings that are convened. That sounds like a lot of work to me. Looking, finding, reading. Who's got the energy?

2. You could option this book. Optioning my book would save you the incalculable grief of trying to ascertain the identity of that one mysterious, magical, super-special book. Think about it: you're reading my book right now, or maybe you're having it read to you by an intern or executive assistant of some sort. Either way, there's no need to make with the fatiguing chore of ordering someone to go do your job for you! Plus, you get the kudos that are conferred only on the executive whose optioned book is developed at virtually no cost to the studio, save for the massive, life-changing optioning fee that *you would have had to pay out anyway*.

Still not convinced? I'll even throw in – at no charge to you! – the catchy tagline that you can apply to the new edition of this book that your corporation's wholly owned subsidiary will market just in advance of when you would have released the film version of this book, if only it had been adaptable in any way whatsoever: *Searching for Michael Jackson's Nose* – Never to be a major motion picture!